The
Phoenix
Transformation

Other books by Brian Tracy
───────────

Entrepreneurship

Get It Done Now!

Make More Money

The Science of Influence

The Science of Money

The Science of Motivation

The
Phoenix
Transformation

12 Qualities of High Achievers to Reboot Your Career and Life

BRIAN TRACY

MEDIA

Published 2021 by Gildan Media LLC
aka G&D Media
www.GandDmedia.com

Front cover design by David Rheinhardt of Pyrographx

Interior design by Meghan Day Healey of Story Horse, LLC

Library of Congress Cataloging-in-Publication Data is available upon request

ISBN: 978-1-7225-1037-4

10 9 8 7 6 5 4 3 2 1

Contents

Preface

The myth of the phoenix is well known. A purplish-red bird, radiant and shimmering, it lives for several hundred years before it dies by bursting into flames. It is then reborn from the ashes to start a new life.

The great Roman poet Ovid tells a slightly different story in his *Metamorphoses*:

> There is a bird, which the Assyrians call the phoenix,
> which renews and reproduces itself.
> It lives, not on fruits or herbs,
> but on drops of incense and cardamom sap.
> When it has lived out the five hundred years of its life,
> with its beak and talons it constructs a nest for itself
> in the branches atop a swaying palm,
> and lines it with cassia and thin stalks of nard, strewn
> with cinnamon flakes and yellow myrrh.
> Thence it is said that a small phoenix, destined to live the
> same number of years, is born from its father's corpse.

When age has given the young one the strength to bear
  its burden,
it relieves the high tree's branches of their weight
and reverently bears its cradle, which was its father's
  tomb,
through the light breezes until it reaches the city of
  Hyperion
and before the sacred gates puts the nest on Hyperion's
  altar.

—Ovid, *Metamorphoses*, 15:392–407
(translated by Richard Smoley)

The phoenix is part of history, too. Tacitus, one of the greatest Roman historians, says that it was seen in Egypt in AD 34 (other ancient sources give the year as 36). Because of the bird's long lifespan, its appearance was thought to herald a new age.

Every age, of course, believes it is a new age, and every age is right—because each one poses its unique situations, difficulties, and opportunities. Ours is no exception.

An old frequently quoted Arab proverb says, "Men resemble their times more than their fathers." This means that in order to survive and prosper, each of us is obliged to understand the times we live in and adapt ourselves to them. Like the phoenix, we may need to reconstitute ourselves for our new age.

In 1983, I produced an audio program called *The Psychology of Achievement*. It's become one of the most popular programs on personal success and achievement in history and has been listened to by over a million people. It's been translated into more than twenty languages, and it has changed the lives of more people than we can count.

The Psychology of Achievement dealt with what I called the inner game of success—how you organize your thoughts, attitudes, and personality and how you set goals, get along with others, understand yourself, and release your personal brakes to accomplish extraordinary things.

Times have changed dramatically since 1983. We have had the introduction of the Internet; we've had the dot-com bubble; we've gone through an accelerating technological revolution; we've been through several different political changes and presidencies. In 1983, China was a backwater. Today it is one of the most booming economies in the world.

Today you often hear people talk about "reinventing themselves." Usually it has to do with their external image—the real or imagined need to make themselves look more hip, more fashionable, and more sophisticated about the latest technological gimmicks and gadgets.

Yes, you do need to reinvent yourself, but changing your image is only a small part of the job—and far from the most important. Do you want results that are different, and better, than you've had in the past? It takes a lot more than getting a new pair of designer glasses. Like the phoenix, you have to renew and restore yourself from the "nest" of the old you.

In this book, I'm going to show you how to do that. I've updated my *Psychology of Achievement* to add cutting-edge research and innovative concepts relevant to the new, wired, and global world we live and work in. *The Phoenix Transformation* contains a series of powerful ideas that I've developed to help you compete in this new world—ideas that you can use to accomplish more in the weeks and months and years ahead than you might have dreamed of in your whole life.

I'm setting out twelve steps to extraordinary achievement—one in each chapter. Are they secrets? No, they're well-known principles, but because so few people use them, they might as well be secrets. Only a tiny minority apply these concepts to their lives. They all have one thing in common: they are successful in every arena.

Twelve Qualities of High Achievers

1. They understand—and use—the power of the mind.
2. They unlock their peak potential by focusing on what they want.
3. They use optimism to motivate themselves to peak performance.
4. They know how to get other people to like and respect them.
5. They set goals and work consistently to achieve them.
6. They organize their time for optimal efficiency.
7. They know how to create wealth for themselves.
8. They are on track to financial independence.
9. They know and use the keys to entrepreneurship.
10. They have mastered self-discipline.
11. They have superb problem-solving skills.
12. They simplify their lives by focusing on the things that give them joy.

1

Change Your Thinking, Change Your Life

Step number one is to key into the most extraordinary source of power you or anyone will ever have: the mind.

I started life humbly. I did not graduate from high school, I bombed out of the twelfth grade, and the only jobs I could get were laboring jobs. My first job was washing dishes in the back of a small hotel. When I lost that job, I got a job washing cars. When I lost that one, I got a job washing floors with a janitorial service. I thought that washing was in my future. But as you can see, it was a downhill trend.

Youth is a euphemism for non-voluntary career redeployment; it's when you get a chance to explore new careers unexpectedly. Today companies have severance programs that give employees to the end of the week or the month. In those days, the severance program was to the end of the hour, and they would fire you at 11:55 or 4:55. They'd come up to you, look at you, grim as death, and say, "Here's your pay, there's the door, and we won't need your services anymore."

I would go from place to place looking for a job. I'd say, "I'm looking for work," and they would say, "We don't need much help right now." I'd say, "I'm the right person for you, because I won't be much help," which wasn't helping my career. I worked as a construction laborer, carrying heavy things from place to place. I worked in sawmills, stacking lumber and trimming boards. One summer I worked digging wells. I worked in the brush with a chainsaw. I worked in a factory, putting on nuts and bolts. I worked on a ship in the North Atlantic. I worked on farms and ranches. At one time, I lived in my car.

When I was twenty-three, I was an itinerant farm laborer, working on a farm during the harvest. I slept on the hay in the farmer's barn. We used to get up at five in the morning, and it was pitch-black. I'd have breakfast with the farmer's family. We had to be out in the fields by the first light so we could get the crop in by the first frost. I was uneducated, I was unskilled, and at the end of the harvest, I was once more unemployed.

The Law of Cause and Effect

When I could no longer get a laboring job, I got a sales job. I got the three-part sales training program: "Here's your cards, here's your brochures, there's the door," and that was it. I went out knocking on doors all day long cold calling, and spun my wheels. I was very frustrated for a long time.

After about six months, I noticed that one guy in our company was making more sales than anybody else by a factor of ten. I went to him and said, "What are you doing differently from me?" He told me, I followed his advice, and my life changed.

From that day on, I began asking, why are some people more successful than others? Why do some people have better lives, earn more money, live in beautiful homes, go to nice restaurants, have lovely vacations? Yet the great majority of people—80 percent, by their own admission—live lives of quiet desperation. They feel that they could be doing far better than they are, but they don't know how.

I eventually found the answers and applied them to my life.

I discovered the law of cause and effect. In sales, the law of cause and effect is very simple: if you do what other successful salespeople do, you get the same results that other successful salespeople get.

Aristotle first discussed this law back around 350 BC, when everybody believed in gods and chance and luck. Aristotle said, "No, no. There's a reason for everything. Everything happens for a reason, whether or not we know the reason; our universe is governed by law."

As I began to study this principle, I made an even more profound discovery—the fact that thoughts are causes, and conditions are effects. Your thoughts create the conditions of your life.

Here is the basic principle that all great men and women eventually discover: *if you change your thinking, you change your life.* If you change the cause, you change the effect. There is no other way. More than any other single factor, the quality of your thinking determines the quality of your life. In fact, you become what you think about most of the time. When you change your thinking, you change your life.

The University of Pennsylvania did a study of 350,000 businesspeople, salespeople, entrepreneurs, and professionals over a twenty-two-year period. These individuals were asked, "What do you think about most of the time?" You know what successful people think about most of the time? The top 10 percent of people in terms of income and income growth think about what they want and how to get it. They think about where they're going and how to get there.

Do you know what unsuccessful people think about most of the time? They think about what they *don't* want, the things that they're worried about, things in the past that make them upset and angry. They especially think about who's to blame for their situation.

Top people think about what they want and how to get it. Average people think about what they don't want and who's to blame.

This insight is like turning a searchlight from one place to another. When you turn your mental searchlight on what you want and how to get it, your whole life begins to change for the better. You begin to revise your thinking by accepting the fact that you are a remarkable person, possessed of incredible abilities and potential, and capable of achieving anything that you want in life.

As I travel around, I meet people who are very successful. I ask them, "What was your childhood like?" They
usually mention a mother or father, or both, who told them
over and over again, "You can do anything you put your
mind to."

That theme rang in these people's young minds. When
they grew up, that was their template: "I can do anything I
put my mind to."

That's what you should say to yourself: "I can do anything I put my mind to. I have unlimited potential."

What you think about most of the time is determined
by your *self-concept*. The discovery of the self-concept was
the greatest psychological breakthrough of the twentieth
century. Your self-concept is the bundle of beliefs about
yourself, your abilities, and your world that determines the
way you see the world around you. You don't see the world
the way it is, but the way you are. You see the world through
your self-concept.

The Self-Concept

Your self-concept is made up of three parts. The first part is
your *self-ideal*: the combination of values, ideals, qualities,
virtues, and goals that you aspire to be, have, or accomplish in the course of your life. In other words, it's how you
imagine yourself as the perfect person—the very best person you could possibly be with the very best qualities you
could possibly have—living the life, and doing and having
the things that are most important to you. This is your self-
ideal. The greater clarity you have about your ideals, the

easier it is for you to make the best decisions in the short term in order to become the kind of person you want to be in the long term.

Superior people—men and women that we admire and look up to—are very clear about their ideals. Unsuccessful, unhappy people are fuzzy about their ideals. Top people will never compromise their ideals and values for anything. Average people will compromise for the slightest advantage or short-term gain. Therefore the starting point of great success, the starting point of shaping your self-concept so that it is consistent with the best person you can possibly be, is to develop clarity about who you are, what you believe in, what you really care about, and what you stand for.

The second part of your self-concept is your *self-image*. This is the way you see yourself and think about yourself in the moment. Your self-image largely determines your performance and effectiveness at a particular task or activity. When you change the way you see yourself, you change your performance and your effectiveness. The person you see is the person you will be.

Psychologists sometimes call your self-image your *inner mirror*: you look into it before you go into a social situation to see how you're expected to behave. When you have a clear picture of yourself performing at your best, you walk in, and you're relaxed, smiling, and confident. Surprise, surprise! Your inner picture becomes your external reality.

Here's an interesting discovery with regard to self-image development: everybody plays a picture in their mind before they go into a situation. Successful people replay the picture of a previous success; unsuccessful people replay a picture of a previous failure. Your subconscious mind doesn't know if you're having a real experience or if you're just having an imaginary experience. If you have a positive experience in some area and you replay it over and over like a continuous reel in your mind, each time you do it, your subconscious records it as a new success experience. Eventually, when you go into a given situation, your subconscious says, "Geez, I've been here before. You are really successful in this area, because I've seen you succeed fifty times." You walk in with a tremendous feeling of confidence, poise, and calmness.

You can always choose the thoughts and pictures that you replay in your mind. Choose to think of your best experiences prior to every event.

The third part of your self-concept is your *self-esteem*. This is the core of your self-concept. Your self-esteem is defined by how much you like yourself. It is the power in your personality. It is the source of your energy, enthusiasm, attitude, personality, and happiness.

Each time you behave in a way that is closer to your self-ideal, your self-esteem goes up. In other words, when you behave as the best person you could possibly be, you like yourself more. When you like yourself more, your self-esteem improves, your personality gets better, you feel happier, you have greater enthusiasm, and you like other people more.

When you set clear goals for yourself and begin working toward them every day, you like and respect yourself more. Your sense of value and personal worth increases.

Your feelings of self-respect and personal pride improve. The very act of setting big goals causes you to like yourself more and to see yourself in a more positive light.

In short, it all comes down to making you think better about yourself, feel better, and perform better in every part of your life. Your basic premises determine the course of your life. Each person has certain ideas about themselves that largely determine the way that they see themselves and their relationship to the world.

Change Your Explanatory Style

Unfortunately, the most common basic premise, and perhaps the worst, is "I'm not good enough": feelings of inadequacy, feelings of incompetence, comparing ourselves unfavorably to others. Feeling deep down that we're not really good enough causes most of our problems and unhappiness.

Psychoanalyst Alfred Adler concluded that each of us has feelings of inferiority. This is not an inferiority complex. A complex is locked in; you can't move it. It's like ink on a white sheet. By contrast, a feeling of inferiority is something that you can change and replace.

People feel inferior to others in some ways, often in many ways. Even if these feelings are not based on fact, they affect our performance. To change your life, the key to improving your outer world is to reprogram your subconscious mind and change your inner world.

The biggest obstacle to maximum performance—happiness, health, and everything you want to accomplish—is your negative emotions. They are mostly based on fear and doubt. They're usually triggered by destructive criticism from one or both parents in early childhood. In fact, you can almost always trace dysfunctionality in an adult back to a dysfunctional childhood, in which the child was criticized and physically or emotionally punished by their parents.

The two negative habit patterns that hold most people back are the fear of failure and the fear of rejection or criticism. Making excuses and blaming other people lie at the root of most negative emotions. You can short-circuit your negative emotions and take control of your self-esteem by accepting 100 percent responsibility for the person you are and everything you accomplish.

The starting point of transforming your thinking is to change your explanatory style—the way you interpret your experience to yourself. Two people could be driving to work, and both could be stuck in a traffic jam. One person could be angry, frustrated, and pounding the steering wheel. The other person could say, "This is an opportunity to think, listen to an educational audio program, and get caught up with the day." Two people, same situation: different explanatory style. When you start explaining things to yourself in a positive way, you start to feel positive about them.

It's never too late to have a happy childhood. This means that the negativity that most people have about their childhood is caught up in the way they interpret it. Imagine that your childhood was sent to you to teach you valuable lessons that you need to know in order to be successful and happy and have a great family when you became an adult. Then you look back on your childhood and say, "Boy, I was lucky that those difficult things happened, because they helped me learn insights that enabled me to be far better with my own family and in my own adult life." You can reinterpret your childhood and make it a happy one just by the way you decide to think about it. You're always free to choose.

Feedback, Not Failure

There is no failure in life, only feedback. Remember, everything happens to you for a reason. If it's a setback, look upon it as feedback: you're getting feedback to help you to self-correct, learn lessons, and move ahead more rapidly and successfully next time. If you look upon every negative experience as a form of feedback that has been sent to help you to be better in the future, you become a more positive and effective person.

In changing your thinking and changing your life, the starting point for you is to dream big dreams.

Here are some questions for you. *What one great thing would you dare to dream if you knew you could not fail?* If you could wave a magic wand and be guaranteed of accomplishing any one goal, short-term or long-term, big or small, what would it be? The answer to this question often tells you what you are put on this earth to do. It often reveals to you your major, definite purpose.

Here's the second question: *What goals would you set for yourself if you had no limitations at all?* I've already talked about basic premises. Some people have a basic premise that they're limited: they're not as creative, they're not as smart, they're not as academically astute, they don't have as high an IQ as others. What if you had all the brains, ability, intelligence, money, friends, and contacts in the world, and you could do, be, or have anything? What goals would you set for yourself? What would you do differently?

Here's the third question. *If you were financially independent today and you could do, be, or have, anything in life, what changes would you make immediately?* Let's say you won the lottery and you're suddenly fabulously wealthy; what immediate changes would you make in your life? Begin thinking about making those changes today, because they are the keys either to the obstacles to your success or to what you were put on this earth to do.

Whatever your answers to these questions may be, write them down. Determine the price you will have to pay to achieve them, and then get busy paying that price. The great oil billionaire H. L. Hunt was once asked, "What are the keys to success?" He said, "The keys to success are, first of all, you have to know exactly what you want. Second, you have to determine the price you'll have to pay. Third, you'll have to resolve to pay that price. Success is very simple. It comes after you've paid the price. First, you do what you have to do, and second, you get the results; it's not the other way around."

Many people say, "As soon as I get the things I want, I'll pay the price." But as inspirational pioneer Earl Nightingale put it, this is like saying to the stove, "As soon as you give me some warmth, I'll put some wood in." That's not the way it works.

By the way, how can you tell how much of the price of success you've already paid? Simple: just look at the conditions of your life. By the law of cause and effect, whatever you've put in, you've gotten out. Whatever you're reaping today is a result of what you've sown in the past.

Decide to Be Rich

You have complete control over what you sow in the present. If you want something different in the future, you have to do something different now. Decide to become rich. People become wealthy because they decide to become wealthy. People worry about money all their lives because they have never decided to become wealthy.

When I discuss money with my audiences, people get a bit offended. I say, "You're poor because you've decided to be poor. People are rich because they've decided to be rich. So if you want to be financially independent, decide to become financially independent."

People reply, "Well, I have."

I say, "No, you haven't made a decision. You've wished and hoped and prayed and read books that tell you it's possible to have riches without working, but you've never made a do-or-die decision to get rich, to become financially independent, because once you do that, you change the direction of your life."

Most millionaires and billionaires today are first-generation wealth: they started with nothing, and by thinking the right thoughts and acting in the right ways, they passed the million-dollar or multi-million-dollar mark in one working lifetime.

Set a goal for yourself to achieve a net worth of $1 million over the next ten or twenty years. Write it down; set a time line that shows you how much you have to acquire each year in order to achieve your goal.

Once you've decided that you want to be worth a million dollars, conduct a complete financial analysis of your current net worth. How much are you worth today? You need to know exactly where you're starting from. Then make a list of twenty different things that you could do, starting immediately, to begin moving toward financial independence. Once you have this list, select one and act on it immediately.

My friend Peter Thomson from England teaches a great exercise: "Imagine that you have reached your deadline, and you're now worth a million dollars. You take a piece of paper and you write at the top of the page, 'I am worth a million dollars today because I . . .' and write down twenty things that you would have done to be worth a million dollars."

This is called *back from the future thinking*. When you do this, you start to think of all the things that you would have done to get to a million dollars, and you get insights and ideas that you would not get through any other exercise.

Read books like *The Millionaire Next Door* and *The Millionaire Mind*. Learn everything you possibly can about how millionaires think, how they decide, how they act. Imagine that you are a millionaire already, and behave accordingly.

Commit to Excellence

Another key to a wonderful life is to *commit to excellence*. Every person who achieved great success in life, both financially and personally, has taken the time and paid the price to become excellent at what they do. According to decades of research, it takes five to seven years for you to achieve mastery in your field, whether you are a neurosurgeon or a diesel mechanic. (It also takes that amount of time to become an excellent salesperson, by the way.) Too many people have a get-rich-quick attitude toward their financial lives. They're always looking for quick, easy ways to shortcut the process of becoming wealthy, but there are no shortcuts that work in the long term.

Ask yourself this question on a regular basis: what one skill, if I developed it in an excellent fashion, would help me the most to achieve my financial goals? What one skill would help me the most in my career, would help me the most to fulfill my dreams?

Whatever your answer is, set excellence in that area as a goal, write it down, make a plan, and then work on becoming better in that area every single day until you achieve that aim.

Sometimes people come up to me and they say that five to seven years is a long time to achieve mastery in their field. Here's a fact: the time is going to pass anyway. At the end of five to seven years, five to seven years will have passed; you'll be five to seven years older. Where are you going to be at the end of those years? Are you going to be at the top of your field, or are you still going to be struggling down in the cheap seats with average people who never make any extra effort to get better? Decide today to join the top 10 percent in your field. Remember, everyone in the top 10 percent started in the bottom 10 percent.

To keep yourself mentally fit, feed your mind regularly with positive materials. Just as you become what you eat, you become what you think about—what you feed into your mind on a regular basis. Read something educational, spiritual, or motivational each day for thirty to sixty minutes. Start your day right, with mental protein in the form of highly nutritious reading rather than mental candy in the form of newspapers and television. If you read thirty to sixty minutes each day in your field, this will amount to about one book per week. One book per week will amount to fifty books per year. If you read fifty books per year in your field, you will get the equivalent of a practical PhD each year. Just reading one hour per day will make you one of the best-educated and highest-paid people in your field within two or three years.

Listen to educational audio programs in your car regularly; never play music or the radio when you're driving from place to place. If you use your car in business, you sit behind the wheel five hundred to a thousand hours each year. This is the equivalent of three months of forty-hour weeks. This is the equivalent of one or two full-time university semesters while just driving from place to place. By listening to educational programs in your car, you can get the equivalent of full-time university attendance in self-directed learning. You can become one of the smartest and most knowledgeable people in your field by turning traveling time into learning time, by turning your car into a mobile classroom, a university on wheels. Attend every course and seminar you possibly can.

Choose the Right People

Associate with other positive, success-oriented people. Get around winners, and stop spending your time with people who are going nowhere with their lives.

To be a great success, put people first. Be selective about the people in your personal life. The people you choose to associate with will have a greater impact on your life and success than perhaps any other factor.

Form a Master Mind group of three to five people who are positive, goal-oriented, and ambitious. Arrange to get together with your Master Mind group for breakfast or lunch at least once per week. Talk about what you are doing and the best ideas you've had in the last week. Share books and articles; help and encourage one another to be even more successful. Napoleon Hill, author of the inspirational classic *Think and Grow Rich*, researched hundreds of wealthy people. He discovered that they only began to fulfill their potential when they formed a Master Mind, meeting regularly with other successful people with positive, optimistic, and creative minds.

Each time you meet with another positive person, you will get ideas, insights, and inspirations that you can use to be happier and more successful. A positive association between two people, a man and a woman, can be the most powerful of all Master Mind groups in achieving success.

Seven Orientations

1. Future orientation
2. Goal orientation
3. Excellence orientation
4. Result orientation
5. Solution orientation
6. Growth orientation
7. Action orientation

Seven Orientations

To change your life, there are seven ways of thinking—or what we can call *orientations*—practiced by the happiest and most successful people. An orientation can be defined as a general tendency of thought: you may get off track on a regular basis, but you keep coming back to this way of thinking. These orientations are practiced by the top 10 percent of people in every field.

The first is *future orientation*. You develop a clear, positive, exciting vision for your future, a five-year fantasy of exactly how you want your life to be in the future. This future vision acts as a powerful motivating force for keeping you positive and forward-thinking. Leaders have vision; non-leaders do not. When you develop an exciting vision for your future, you become a leader in your own life.

The second orientation is *goal orientation*. You become goal-oriented by making a list of ten goals that you would like to accomplish in the next year. Select the most important goal from that list. Make a plan for its accomplishment, and then work on your plan every single day until it's achieved. This one exercise will change your life, and I'll talk about it at greater length later.

The third orientation is *excellence orientation*. Resolve today to be the best at what you do. Join the top 10 percent in your field. Select the one skill that can help you more than any other skill today, and commit yourself to becoming excellent in that one area. Get better one skill at a time.

The fourth is *result orientation*. In the final analysis, you are always and only paid for the results that you get for other people. Plan every day with a list. Organize your list by priority. Always concentrate on the most valuable use of your time. Ask yourself continually, "What can I, and only I, do that will make a real difference in my life?" Work on that single-mindedly.

The fifth orientation is *solution orientation*. Life is a series of problems, difficulties, challenges, reverses, setbacks, and temporary failures. The way you respond to these ups and downs will largely determine your success and happiness. Always focus on solutions rather than problems. The more you think and talk about the solutions, the more solution-oriented you will be, and the more solutions you will come up with to solve the problems that arise as you move toward your goal.

The sixth orientation is *growth orientation*. Dedicate yourself to lifelong learning. To earn more, you must learn more. Invest at least as much in your mind each year as you do in your car. If you spend as much on getting better in your field as you invest in your car, you're going to be rich, happy, and successful.

The seventh orientation, which is the key to everything, is *action orientation*. Action is everything. Develop a sense of urgency. Move fast on opportunities and problems. Develop a bias for action. Be in continual motion toward your goals. Keep saying to yourself over and over again: "Do it now. Do it now. Do it now."

You are a potential genius. Your job is to unlock your mental powers by continually thinking and talking about the things you want and the direction you are going in. Refuse to think or talk about things that make you unhappy or about problems and difficulties. Develop the habit of focusing single-mindedly on your most important goals, tasks, and activities. Think and talk in terms of solutions and opportunities, and above all, take continuous action all day, every day, toward what you really want in your life.

2

Unlocking Your Potential

You have more potential within you than you could use in a hundred lifetimes. And the more of your potential you use, the more is available to you. You really have no idea what you're capable of accomplishing until you begin to stretch yourself. Perhaps your most important responsibility in life—to yourself and to others—is to use your full potential for happiness, success, and achievement.

In this chapter, I will share with you some of the very best ideas used by the happiest and most successful people in the world to get the most out of themselves.

There's never been a better time in all of human history to be alive. Regardless of short-term ups and downs in the economy and politics, at this wonderful time in history you have the ability to be, do, and have, more than you ever had before.

Three Exercises

Here are three quick exercises. Number one: imagine that you have the ability to double or triple your income or even increase it by ten times in the years ahead.

Sometimes when I'm talking to an audience, I say, "Everybody here worries about money. Imagine that I could wave a magic wand and double the income of everyone in this room. Would that solve your financial problems?"

People say, "Yes, yes."

"How about if I could triple your income?"

"Yes, yes."

"How about if I could increase your income five or ten times?"

"Yes, yes, yes."

"Now let me ask you a question: how many people here, from the time you took your first job until today, have already doubled their incomes?"

Every hand in the room goes up. If I ask whether they have tripled their incomes, 80 percent of the hands go up. The room is full of hands even when I ask them if they multiplied their incomes five or ten times.

In other words, you've already achieved these things in the past, and if you've achieved them in the past, you know how to do it again in the future.

Number two: Imagine having perfect health and fitness in every respect. Imagine you could wave a magic wand and be superbly fit and healthy in every respect. What would it look like? How would you feel?

Number three, which is perhaps the most important: imagine having perfect relationships and a wonderful family life in every way: full of love, harmony, joy, peace, and laughter. How would it be different from today?

Einstein said, "Imagination is more important than facts." Inspirational speaker Denis Waitley said, "Your imagination is your preview of life's coming attractions." The more exciting your imagination is, the higher your self-esteem. The better your self-image, the greater your self-ideal, the more confident and positive you are overall as a person.

Practice the magic wand technique in every area of your life. Imagine that you could wave a magic wand in the areas of income, health, and relationships, and have three wishes in each area. What would you wish for? All success in life begins with an exciting vision of what is possible for you. In order to create a vision, you must unleash the power of your imagination.

"I Like Myself"

The greatest breakthrough in the development of human potential, as I've already said, is the discovery of the self-concept.

Your self-concept precedes and predicts your levels of effectiveness in anything you do. It determines how you perform on the outside. All improvement in your life begins with an improvement in your self-concept, with an improvement of how you think about yourself.

Your self-concept is your bundle of beliefs about yourself. It's all the beliefs that you have about yourself, starting back in early childhood. This bundle of beliefs is largely subjective: it's not a fact. It's based on information that you have taken in and accepted as true, especially about yourself and your own abilities.

Your self-esteem, the most important part of your personality, your emotional center, is best defined as how much you like yourself.

You can change your self-concept, boost your self-esteem, improve your self-image, and move more rapidly toward your goals and dreams by repeating over and over the words: *I like myself. I like myself. I like myself.*

An ecstatically happy woman came up to me once. She said that when she first heard this from me, she spent two years trying to say, *I like myself*, but because of all the negativity with which she had been burdened from childhood, she couldn't. One day she woke up and said, "I love myself. I love myself." The dam broke, and the sun came out. She's been a happy person ever since.

The best thing you can say when you get up in the morning is, *I like myself. I like myself. I like myself.* Before you go into a meeting of any kind, get yourself psychologically pumped: *I like myself. I like myself. I like myself.* It's amazing how much happier you'll feel and how much more you'll like other people as a result.

Now the great rule for success is that everything counts. Everything you do either helps or hurts. Everything either moves you toward your goals or moves you away from them. Everything builds up your self-esteem or tears it down. Psychologists say that everything we do in life is either to build our self-esteem or to protect it. So you must be alert to the facts: the things that you do, the books you read, the people you associate with, the conversations you have. Do they raise or lower your self-esteem?

The Benefits of Self-Esteem

There are a number of great benefits of self-esteem. Number one is, the more you like yourself, the better you do at everything you attempt. Psychology has discovered that self-esteem is the flip side of the coin of self-efficacy. What does that mean? It means the better you do something, the more you like yourself. The more you like yourself, the better you do it. As you raise your self-esteem, your competence, your performance, your ability improves simultaneously.

The second benefit is, the more you like yourself, the more you like others, and the more they like you. The more you like yourself, the more you'll like the members of your family. Parents with high self-esteem raise children with high self-esteem. High self-esteem children grow up and marry other high self-esteem children, they in turn give you high self-esteem grandchildren, and have high self-esteem lives. It's like the warmth of a fire spreading out: your self-esteem has a positive effect on others.

This factor is especially important in sales, communication, persuasion, and negotiation. In sales, there's a one-to-one relationship between your level of self-esteem and your level of sales. The higher your self-esteem, the more you'll sell in any market. Why? It's because people buy things from people they like. And the more they like you, the more they want to buy from you, and they'll buy again and recommend you to their friends.

In communication, persuasion, and negotiation, the more we like a person, the more open we are to being influenced by that person. The more you like yourself, the bigger goals you will set, and with greater confidence. The more you like yourself, the longer you persist, and the faster you bounce back from adversity.

High self-esteem enriches every part of your life. You'll have high levels of optimism and a positive mental attitude. You'll approach life differently than you would with low self-esteem. You'll have high levels of self-confidence and courage.

The things that hold us back are the great fears: fears of failure, of rejection. It's like a teeter-totter: the higher your self-esteem, the lower your fears; the more you like yourself, the less you fear failure and the less you feel criticism. The more you like yourself, the more willing you are to try different things because you know that temporary failures or disapproval don't reflect on your value at all.

Another key benefit is that high self-esteem leads to a positive, popular, likable personality. The more you like yourself, the more positive and optimistic you are, the more cheerful you are, the more energy you have, the more people like you and want to be around you socially and in business.

The Seven Mental Laws

1. The law of cause and effect
2. The law of control
3. The law of belief
4. The law of expectation
5. The law of attraction
6. The law of correspondence
7. The law of superconscious activity

The Seven Mental Laws

Seven mental laws determine your life and your potential. The first, which I mentioned earlier, is the *law of cause and effect*. It says that everything happens for a reason. We live in a universe governed by law, not by chance. Success is not an accident; neither is failure.

The law of cause and effect says that if you do what successful people do, you must ultimately enjoy the same success that they enjoy. There's no other way. The world is full of people who are doing what failures do, and they're surprised that they're getting the results that failures get. If you want to be successful, find out what successful people do, and do that over and over again, without deviation, until you achieve the same result.

Again, the most important application of the law of cause and effect is that thoughts are causes, and conditions are effects. Thought is creative; it creates your life. Your thoughts create the conditions of your life. If you want to create new conditions in your external life, you must create new thinking on the inside.

The second law is the *law of control*. It says that you feel positive about yourself to the degree to which you feel you are in control of your own life.

You can have either an internal locus of control or an external locus of control. An internal locus means that you feel that you're in charge, you make your own decisions—you're in the driver's seat, and you determine what happens to you. An external locus of control comes from feeling that you don't have any control. You're passive, you're a victim, you're controlled by what other people want and say, your past experiences, your bills, or your current situation.

Stress comes from feeling that you are controlled by outside people and circumstances. Happiness and high performance come from feeling that you are in control of your life.

When you live by the law of control, you take complete control over everything that happens to you, which brings us to an interesting observation: there's only one thing in the world over which you have complete control, and that is your thinking. Fortunately, you are designed by nature so that if you take complete control over your thinking, you take complete control over everything else as well.

The third law that determines your potential is the *law of belief*. It is the foundation of all religions, philosophies, and metaphysics. It says that your intensely held beliefs become your realities. The law of belief says that you always act in a manner consistent with what you believe.

Your beliefs determine your actions, and your actions determine your results.

Worst of all are self-limiting beliefs that are not based on fact. They are basic premises that you have accepted about yourself and your potential that are not true. Have you ever thought you weren't particularly good at something and then tried it out and found out that you had a natural ability in that area? Prior to that, you were holding a false belief.

Many people have false beliefs that hold them back all their lives. One multimillionaire said that when he was growing up, his father would say over and over, "People in our family are working people. People in our family never achieve financial success. We work for a living all our lives. We've always been blue-collar workers."

This man accepted these beliefs when he was growing up. He left high school without making much of an effort. The first job he got was working as a laborer. One day, two or three years after getting out of high school, he was digging a ditch on a highway crew. Traffic was moving very slowly next to him. As it moved up, he saw someone he had gone to high school with. That guy was not very smart and didn't get very good grades, yet there he was, driving a new car.

This man was talking to his old classmate while standing there with a shovel: "Hi, Bill. How are you?"

"Hi, Sam. How's it going?"

"What are you doing now?"

"Oh, I got this job and I'm doing well. I got a new car. I'm getting a house in a couple of months."

The man looked at his old classmate, and it hit him like a door slammed in his face. He realized he had bought a bill of goods from his father. He had bought his father's beliefs and premises. Here was this guy, having a great life, and here he was, digging ditches in the hot sun. He threw the shovel into the ditch, got up, walked out, and said, "I'm going to do what you do." A few years later, he was a multimillionaire. The turning point in his life came when he challenged the negative, self-limiting beliefs that were holding him back.

Number four is the *law of expectation*. It says that whatever you expect with confidence becomes your own self-fulfilling prophecy. There are libraries full of books on what is called *expectations theory*. Basically, they say the entire stock market moves on the basis of expectations. The people we marry, the jobs we take, the goals we set for ourselves, and our courses of endeavor are also based on certain sets of expectations. Negative expectations accompany underachievement and failure; positive expectations accompany success and achievement.

You get not what you want in life, but what you expect. The rule is always to expect the best in every situation. Expect the best from each person that you meet, but most of all, expect the best from yourself.

The fifth law is the *law of attraction*, which says that you are a living magnet. You invariably attract into your life people and circumstances that are in harmony with your dominant thoughts.

Recently a lot has been written and said about the law of attraction. It's one of more than thirty laws that determine your life. It's very helpful, but it is not the only law, nor is it the most important. Basically, it says that if you can think about something with intense emotion and great clarity, keep your mind on it, and work toward it every day, you start to attract into your life people and circumstances that help move you ahead faster.

The sixth law is the *law of correspondence*. Almost everything I've studied over the last thirty years comes back to this law. It says that your outer world tends to correspond to your inner world like a mirror image. Wherever you look, there you are. Your job is to create an inner world that is consistent with the outer world that you wish to enjoy.

The great metaphysician Emmet Fox wrote a little pamphlet some years ago called *The Mental Equivalent*. It says that your primary job in life is to provide the mental equivalent of what you want to enjoy on the outside. All the powers of nature and the universe will come together to help you create that mental equivalent, but you must have a clear picture on the inside of what you want to have in your outer life, and everything will start to take place after that.

The Bible says that according to your faith, it is done unto you. Another saying teaches, as within, so without. When you're clear about what you want, your outer world begins to mirror it in three areas. First of all, in your relationships. How you think and feel about yourself is projected out and determines the people that you're associated with and attracted to. Your inner world will also be reflected in your lifestyle, the conditions of your life, and your income. Your inner preparation determines the amount that you earn. Of course, your inner world of thinking and acting determines your health and fitness. The starting point is to go back to the drawing board and begin working on the mental equivalent that is creating the world around you.

The last law is my favorite: the *law of superconscious activity*: any thought, plan, goal, or idea that is held continuously in your conscious mind must be brought into reality by your superconscious mind. In other words, because of this great power in the universe, you can have anything that you can hold in your mind on a continuing basis.

Here are the characteristics of the superconscious mind that make it so powerful: First, once you have provided your superconscious mind with your goals it works continuously on them twenty-four hours a day. Second, your superconscious mind solves every problem on the way to your goal, as long as your goal is clear. When you have an obstacle or difficulty or challenge, a door opens. You come across a piece of information; you have an idea or insight; you have an intuition or gut feeling; as you move toward your goal, every problem is solved in order.

Third, your superconscious mind brings you exactly the answer you require at exactly the right time for you. I've had experiences where I've been in a tremendous dilemma, and I was going into a very serious meeting. As I walked across the doorstep, the perfect answer came to me. I said it, and the whole situation resolved itself.

The superconscious will bring you the answer that you require, but here's the rule: a superconscious answer is time dated. You must act on it immediately. If you're driving along, and you get an intuition to phone somebody, you should pull over and act on it immediately. If you're looking at a book and you feel you should buy it, grab it. If you're looking at a magazine and feel you should read an article, read it. If you see somebody you feel you should introduce yourself to, introduce yourself—because often that is the turning point in your life.

Fourth, your superconscious mind requires clear goals to work on, preferably in writing. In fact, you really do not know or understand something unless you can write it down clearly.

If you cannot write down an idea, making the connection from the head to the hand, you probably don't understand it. Your superconscious mind cannot go to work on your goal unless you can write it out with crystal clarity.

Your goal should be so clear that a child could read it and explain it exactly to another child. A child should be able to read your goal and tell you if you've accomplished it or how close you are to attaining it. If your goal is not written with such clarity that a child could understand it, you need to go back to work on it. The simpler your goal is, and the greater clarity with which it is expressed in writing, the faster all of your mental powers go to work to bring it into your life.

Fifth, your superconscious mind is activated by visualization and positive commands from your conscious mind to your subconscious mind, especially the words, *I like myself.* Whenever you think of your goal and you say, *I like myself, I like myself*, it activates your mental powers.

Sixth, your superconscious mind operates best with a mental attitude of calm, confident expectation. You probably know people who say when things go wrong, "Oh, don't worry, something will turn up. Everything will be all right, everything will be OK." Surprise, surprise—for these people, something always turns up; something is always OK. The more calmly confident you are that everything will be fine, the more rapidly your goal will appear in your life.

Finally, number seven: your superconscious mind releases ideas and energy for goal attainment on a continuing basis. When you are working toward something that's really important to you, you seem to have a continuous flow of energy and ideas. Sometimes you can work long hours without being fatigued. When you're really excited about something you're working on, you can work sixteen-hour days, seven days a week, and you don't need to sleep, because your superconscious mind is a source of free energy. This is energy that you can attract to yourself from the universe that drives you toward your goal. It also gives you all kinds of ideas and insights that make it possible.

Goal orientation is the key to unlocking your potential, causing all of these mental laws to work on your behalf and move you toward you what you desire. You don't have to think about the laws, because when you have a clear goal, the law of cause and effect goes to work. The cause is your thoughts about your goals, and the effect is moving toward them. The law of control then goes to work. How do you control your thinking? You think about your goals. The law of belief goes to work once you believe that everything you're doing is moving you toward your goals. The law of expectations starts when you expect that everything that happens will help you achieve your goals. The law of attraction allows you to continually attract people, circumstances, and ideas to achieve your goal. Then the law of correspondence—how your outer world corresponds with your goals. And of course, the law of superconscious activity, working twenty-four hours a day, moves you more and more rapidly toward your goals and moves them toward you. Goals:

- Release ideas and energy, unlocking your potential.
- Improve your self-concept, raise your self-esteem, and make you like yourself more.
- Increase your self-confidence and make you unstoppable in the pursuit of your goals.

I'll explain more about setting and achieving goals in chapter 5.

The 1,000 Percent Formula

I want to show you how to increase your productivity, performance, and income by 1,000 percent—by ten times in the years ahead. I call this the *1,000 percent formula.* It's based on the law of incremental improvement, which says that people get better little by little. Nobody goes immediately from being average or mediocre to being outstanding. Remember, it takes five to seven years for you to excel in your field, to achieve mastery, to be in the top 10 percent. Since it takes a long time, you better get started.

The 1,000 percent formula is also based on the law of accumulation. The law of accumulation says that success is the result of hundreds and even thousands of small efforts and sacrifices that no one ever sees or appreciates.

There's a wonderful line from Henry Wadsworth Longfellow: "Those heights by great men (and women) reached and kept, were not achieved by sudden flight, but they, while their companions slept, were toiling upward in the night." While most people are watching television, socializing, and having fun, the people who are going to be great in the future are busy working away and expanding their knowledge. They're getting better a little bit at a time. The key to success is simple: get a little better every single day—continuous and never-ending improvement.

Here's the question: could you increase your productivity, performance, and output by 0.1 percent in a day? Could you start a little earlier, work a little harder, stay a little later, focus on higher priorities, and become 1/1000 more productive in a day?

I ask my audiences this question, and everybody says, "Sure. You could do that in thirty seconds." I say, "Well, having done it for the first day, could you do it for the second day?" They say yes. How about the third day, fourth day, fifth day? They say yes, so you could do it for a whole week. Well, 0.1 percent times five days is 0.5 percent. Could you become 0.5 percent more productive over the next week if you really wanted to? People say, "Of course." Having done it for the first week, could you do it for the second? People say yes. How about the third and the fourth week? They say yes.

Something interesting starts to happen here: it's called the *momentum principle*. You get into the rhythm of it. It's like getting up in the morning and exercising: it gets easier and easier. Having done that for the first week, could you do it for the second week, the third, and the fourth week? That works out to 2 percent in a month.

Could you continue to improve for the second, third, and fourth month? People say yes. That means you could do it for an entire year. Now there are 13 4-week months in a year—52 weeks. Improving by 2 percent per month times 13 equals 26 percent over the course of a year.

Is it possible for you—by working on yourself, managing your time better, and focusing and concentrating on high-value tasks—to become 26 percent more productive in the course of a single year? The answer is yes, of course. If you really wanted to, you could be twice as productive in a month, so 26 percent a year is reasonable. Having done it for the first year, could you do it the second year? Of course. The third year and the fourth year? Yes.

If you increase your productivity, performance, and output by 26 percent per year, you will increase your income by the same amount. Consequently, you will double your productivity, performance, and income in 2.7 years. Compounded over 10 years, that will give you an increase of 1,004 percent in your productivity, performance, output, and income.

This is the most remarkable thing: simply by getting 0.1 percent better per day, 0.5 percent better for 5 days, 2 percent better per month, 26 percent better per annum, you'll become 10 times better and more highly paid in the course of a decade.

I was at a seminar in Seattle recently, and a young friend of mine named Chris came up to me. He said, "It's been seven years since I took your seminar. I've practiced your

1,000 percent formula every day, and it doesn't work." I said, "What do you mean?" He said, "Well, I've gotten up every day, I've done the seven things that you recommend every single day, and your formula doesn't work. I didn't increase my income ten times in ten years."

"Really?"

Then he smiled and said, "I increased my income ten times in seven years. This year I made ten times what I was earning when I first met you. It's the most remarkable thing I ever heard of. It transformed my life. It's enabled me to have a fabulous life for my family, live in a beautiful house, have my kids in private schools. It's absolutely wonderful."

Here are the seven ingredients of the 1,000 percent formula.

1. Each morning, arise two hours before you have to be at work or an appointment, and for thirty to sixty minutes, read something that's educational, motivational, or inspirational. Best of all, read on how to be better at your current job. As I've already mentioned, reading for thirty to sixty minutes a day is a book a week. A book a week is fifty books a year; fifty books a year is five hundred books in ten years. (At the very least, you'll need a bigger house just to hold your books.) Now if all you did were to read one hour, every single day, in your field, that alone would increase your income 1,000 percent over the next ten years.

2. Rewrite and review your major goals each morning before you start off. I suggest that you get a spiral note-

book. At the top of the page, write today's date, and write down your ten goals every day. This reprograms them into your subconscious mind, activating your superconscious powers and setting you off on your day with great clarity about what you're trying to accomplish.

If all you do is rewrite and review your major goals each morning, that alone will increase your income ten times in the next ten years.

3. Plan every day in advance; make a list the night before. Again, if all you did was to meticulously plan every day in advance, that would increase your productivity, performance, and output by 25 percent. The first day you start doing it, that will give you your year's growth in productivity in the first day. If you just do that every day, that will increase your income by ten times in ten years.

4. Set priorities on your tasks, and concentrate on the most valuable use of your time all day long. This is the greatest of all success principles: to identify the most important thing you could be doing, and do only that all day long. That will have more of an impact on your life than you can imagine. That alone will increase your income ten times in ten years.

5. Listen to podcasts or audio programs in your car. Everywhere I go all over the world, I meet people who began to listen to them and became addicted. They listened to programs about goals and time management and rela-

tionships, and selling and business and financial accumulation. They say they became completely different people, because as you listen, that information is programmed into your subconscious mind.

Over and over people have said to me, "I was in a certain situation, and I didn't know what to do; then I remembered the words from a program, said the words, or I did what the words said to do, and I got the result I expected." You can never tell where great ideas are going to come from, so you have to take in a lot of good ideas.

I met a young man in St. Louis recently who said he was not a great reader but was a good listener. He came to my program. He wanted to get all six of my programs, but he didn't have the money. He ran home, borrowed the money from his mother at a lunch break, came back, and bought them. When he got the programs, he was driving an old car, living at home, and had little or no money.

"This year, four years later, I made more than $500,000," he said. "I have a brand-new car, I have a beautiful home; I'm married; I'm happy. I've never had more money in my life. My income keeps going up every year. I attribute all of this to listening to those programs. It's the only influence on my life that was different from what I was doing before."

Does it work? Yes. Sometimes people say to me, "Yeah, but what if it doesn't work?" What if it does? Can you afford *not* to give it a try? Just listening to audio programs will increase your income ten times in the next ten years.

6. After every experience, ask the two magic questions which enable you to unlock more of your potential, become smarter faster, and answer your questions more than any others I've ever learned.

Question number one is, *What did I do right?* If you make a sales call or a presentation, immediately afterward do a debriefing and ask, "What did I do right?" I used to sit down with a pad and paper and write down everything I'd done right, because obviously I had done some things right, no matter how the situation worked out.

The second question is, *What would I do differently next time if I had this to do over?* Write down all the ways that you could improve your performance.

Notice the special quality of these two questions: the answers are both positive. Many people used to think that when you make a mistake, you should immediately dissect it and ask, "Where did I go wrong?" But whatever you reflect upon, whatever you imagine and discuss and recall, you are reprogramming into your subconscious mind. If you go over your mistakes, you're reprogramming yourself to make more mistakes in similar situations in the future.

If instead you recall all the things you did right and all the things you could do better next time, you program them into your subconscious mind, and you predispose yourself to do them right the next time.

Always ask those two questions: What did I do right? What would I do differently?

7. Treat every person you meet like a million-dollar customer, beginning with the members of your family and extending outward from there. Remember, every person considers themselves to be the most important person in the world. When you acknowledge that by treating them as if they had the ability to buy a million dollars of your product or service, they will treat you with the same warmth, affection, and respect.

You'll find that all of the highest paid people in every industry are liked by their clients and customers. Why? Because they treat their clients and customers like special and important people.

Three Keys to Your Potential

Here are three final keys to unlocking your potential:

1. Decide exactly what you want. You can't hit a target that you can't see.
2. Set priorities, and work on your most valuable tasks every single day.
3. Resolve in advance that you won't give up until you achieve the goals you set for yourself.

Keep reminding yourself of those wonderful words: *failure is not an option.* As the great inventor Thomas Edison said, "When you have exhausted all possibilities, remember this: you haven't."

3

Motivating Yourself to Peak Performance

We've gone through two steps now in the Phoenix Transformation. First, you learned that the greatest power that you possess, or anyone possesses, is the mind. You change your reality when you change your mind. Then you learned that you can gain access to this amazing power through methods such as visualizing what you want and setting clear, concrete goals based on it.

Now let's concentrate on peak performance—getting the best out of yourself. The average person works at less than fifty percent of capacity. Consequently, by motivating yourself, you can get far more out of yourself and your life.

Motivation is very much like mental health. Physical health requires you to do physical exercises; similarly, mental health—personal motivation—requires you to do mental exercises.

You have the potential right now to be more, do more, and have more than ever before. No matter what you've accomplished so far in life, it's only a small part of what is possible for you.

Superior people believe that the future is going to be better than the past. They believe that the future is going to be the greatest time of their lives. They believe that their days of highest income lie ahead of them and that their greatest achievements are still to come. They believe that their happiest and most loving moments are still in the future. They have an attitude toward life that kids have toward Christmas: "I can hardly wait." Because of the law of expectations, their lives get better and better.

Use Your Imagination

The average person uses only 10 percent or less of his or her mental potential. This means that by unlocking more of your existing talents and abilities, you could achieve double, triple, and even five or ten times what you're achieving today.

Start by imagining that you could double your income in the next year or two: how much would that be? Write it down as a goal and begin thinking about that number every day. You will almost immediately start getting ideas and opportunities to double your income.

Here's the second exercise: imagine increasing your income by ten times. Just add a zero to your current income to get that number. Now here's what I've discovered over the years. If you say, "I'm earning $50,000 a year today, so if I add one zero, that's $500,000." Just as your body will reject a new organ, your mind will reject that idea. It will kick it back out and say, "Absolutely not; it's impossible," because your brain cannot take such an incredible change. So you push it back in again and say, "Well, just imagine I could earn $500,000." Your mind will kick it out again, but just keep saying, "X to 10X. X is my current income: $50,000. Ten Xs, $500,000. X to 10X." As you keep thinking that—"50 to 500, 50 to 500"—eventually your brain will get tired and stop kicking it out. At a certain point it will say, "Oh, all right, maybe it's possible."

Then your superconscious mind kicks in and says, "Maybe if you just did this, maybe that would help a little bit." Then the dam starts to break, and you get all kinds of ideas that increase your income from $50,000 to $55,000, $55,000 to $60,000, and $60,000 to $70,000.

Things begin to happen, but they happen slowly. Don't expect lightning to flash and suddenly it will be accomplished. Expect these changes to happen incrementally as you get your mind around the idea of earning double or triple or ten times what you're earning today.

Now here's a good question: are these numbers possible? Of course they're possible. Thousands and millions of people are already earning these amounts. They all started out earning less than you are earning today. You know something? Nobody's smarter than you; nobody's better than you. They are just doing different things in a different way.

I've been astonished. I've met average people doing things in an above average way who are earning five and ten times as much as I am. I just shake my head about how that can be possible. Then I look at what they're doing: they're doing something different in a different field. They know more about what they're doing than I do, and they're concentrating on the one thing that they know. I have met people whose IQs I'd say didn't reach room temperature but who are earning more money than me. Why? It's because they don't try to be good at large numbers of things. They just tried to be really good at one thing and do it over and over again.

Is it possible? Of course it is. The greatest discovery in history is that you become what you think about most of the time. The key to high levels of self-esteem, self-respect, and self-confidence is to think about yourself in positive terms most of the time. You also become what you say to yourself most of the time: your self-talk, your inner dialogue, determines 95 percent of your emotions.

Overcome the Default Setting

Now here's an important fact: if you don't consciously and deliberately talk to yourself in a positive way, you default automatically to negative thinking.

Do you think about your worries and problems, and the people and situations you're mad at? If you're not careful, you will resort to the automatic default setting: stinking thinking. You have to keep your mind on what you want and how to get it. Focus on positive things for an extended period of time. If you do something over and over again, you eventually develop a habit. Pretty soon you develop the habit of always thinking positively and constructively about yourself and your life.

Every day, talk to yourself positively by saying things like *I like myself* or *I can do it* or *I'm the best*. As businessman and inspirational thinker W. Clement Stone used to teach, say the words *I feel happy, I feel healthy, I feel terrific*.

Wonderfully—because your conscious mind can only hold one thought at a time—if you keep repeating these words, they start to become your reality. You reprogram yourself internally with a new mental equivalent.

An important key to self-motivation and self-confidence is to cancel out negative thoughts and feelings. Nature abhors a vacuum. If you eliminate negative thoughts and feelings from your mind, you create a mental vacuum, and nature fills it with positive thoughts and feelings.

As I've already mentioned, two main fears trigger the negative emotions that hold you back. Number one is the fear of failure. This is the biggest single obstacle to success in adult life. It's the fear of loss—loss of money, loss of time, loss of love—it's the fear of poverty. We all have this fear, usually going back to early childhood.

The second major fear is the fear of rejection: the fear of criticism, embarrassment, ridicule, or the opinions of others. Do you know that 54 percent of adults fear public speaking more than death? You know why? Because they're afraid of embarrassment. They're afraid that if they stand up and speak, people will laugh at them; they'd rather die than stand up and speak.

These fears are very big: they have an enormous impact on our lives. Both of them are learned in childhood as a result of destructive criticism from one or both parents. Yet because these fears were learned, they can be unlearned. This is the miracle of modern psychology. Fears can be unlearned by using the *law of substitution*. The law of substitution says your mind can only hold one thought at a time, positive or negative. You can deliberately substitute a positive thought for a negative thought. Many people have told me that this in itself changed their lives. They didn't realize they had so much control. They didn't realize that they could choose to replace a negative thought with a positive thought and do it over and over again until the positive thought locked in or set like concrete.

Both the fear of failure and the fear of rejection can be canceled by saying the words *I like myself*. The more you like yourself, the less you fear failure; the more you like yourself, the less you fear rejection, criticism, and the comments of other people.

As your self-esteem goes up, your fears go down. You can cancel the fear of failure in particular by repeating the words *I can do it* over and over: *I can do it, I can do it*. You see, the fear of failure is summarized in the feeling *I can't, I can't, I can't*. This *I can't* holds us back from trying something new, from taking risks. Whenever you have a fear of cold calling, of knocking on doors, of taking a chance, say to yourself over and over again, *I can do it, I can do it, I can do it, I can do it*. As you say this, your confidence goes up and your fears go down.

Now here's an interesting discovery. In psychology, it's called the *boomerang effect*. Everything you do or say that makes another person feel better about themselves causes you to feel better about yourself as well.

If you have people in your family or your social circle whom you want to influence in a positive way, always tell them, *you can do it, you can do it, you can do it*. Encourage people; don't tell them all the reasons why it won't work. Many people in life will do that. Always encourage people by telling them that they can do it, instead. Sometimes you can change a person's entire life by encouraging them—putting courage into them by telling them, *you can do it*. They'll come up later and say, "You know, I was really unsure, I was really insecure, but when you told me I could do it, I said, 'Well, what the heck,' and it changed my whole life." As you encourage others and raise their courage, you feel better and more confident yourself. One hand washes the other.

Mental Cross-Training

The most important quality for self-esteem and self-motivation is optimism. The top 10 percent of people in any field are optimists. They believe in themselves. They see everything that happens—every setback, every difficulty, every challenge—as an opportunity of some kind.

Optimism is like mental fitness. It's the measure of mental health and of a positive personality. If you want to be physically fit, you go to the gym and you work out. If you want to become mentally fit, you do mental cross-training. Here are four keys to optimism, to mental cross-training.

1. Think and talk about what you want and how to get it, because whatever you think and talk about, you're going to draw into your life.

   You must be very careful. Sometimes my wife, Barbara, and I are talking about something that went wrong at work or in investments. Barbara will say, "Hey, wait a minute. Do we want more of this in our life?" I'll say, "No." Then we stop talking about it.

   This is called a *pattern interrupt*: to stop talking about something that is turning over in your mind, just say the word *stop* very hard. This gives you a kind of face slap and stops the thinking pattern. Then immediately replace this thought by thinking about your goals.

   In fact, one of the most wonderful ways to keep yourself optimistic is to think about your goals. Whenever you are cut off in traffic, think about your goals. Whenever you're worried about something, think about your goals. Whenever you have a problem, think about your goals. As you go through your daily life, think and talk about what you want and how to get it. As you do that, you become more and more positive and optimistic.

2. The second key to optimism is to look for the good in every situation. Whenever something goes wrong—whenever you have a problem—immediately stop and say, "Well, that's good"; then go into the situation and find out what is good.

When you look for something good in every diffi-culty, you always find it. You can think of this in terms of a dimmer switch. You manually control it your dim-mer switch: you either turn it up or down. If you turn it up, your lights will be bright. If you turn it down, your lights will be low.

You also have a dimmer switch on your brain. It's controlled by your thoughts. When your mental dim-mer switch is up, you're positive, you're creative, you're happy, you have high energy, and you have a great sense of humor; you're the best person you can possibly be. When your dimmer switch is on low, you're negative, you're angry, you're worried, you're fearful. Your job is to keep your dimmer switch on full most of the time, but how do you do that? Whenever you think and talk about what you want, or whenever you look for the good in a situation, your dimmer switch goes on full, and you become positive and creative.

3. Seek the valuable lesson in every problem. Successful people realize that every problem, difficulty, setback, or obstacle contains a valuable lesson that can help them to be even more successful in the future. My late friend Norman Vincent Peale, author of *The Power of Positive Thinking*, once said, "When God wants to send you a gift, he wraps it up in a problem. The bigger the gift that God wants to send you, the bigger the problem he wraps it up in."

You may feel as if it's Christmas morning around your house, with lots of gifts all over the place, but every problem or difficulty that you have contains a gift of some kind.

Imagine that there's a great power in the universe that wants you to be successful and happy in the future. This great power knows that you have a perverse nature: you will not learn the lessons you need to learn to be successful until it hurts. Therefore this great power sends you lessons on a regular basis. Each one is accompanied by pain of some kind. It could be physical pain, financial pain, or emotional pain, but it's always accompanied by pain, and the pain is to get your attention.

Whenever you are experiencing anything that is causing you pain, anxiety, or distress, ask, "What is the lesson contained in this situation? What am I meant to learn here?" If you look, you will always find one or more lessons. Great souls are those who learn great lessons from small events.

Some people have to be beaten over the head several times before they learn the lesson. When other people experience a pain, they say, "A lesson coming down the pike; I wonder what it is."

As you look for the lesson, your dimmer switch goes on full, and you become a positive person. When you look for a lesson in every problem, you will always find something. Sometimes the lesson can make you successful. Many times you will look back and say, "Thank heavens that happened earlier, because it taught me that lesson, which enabled me to be successful and happy in this situation today." Always take the high road and look for the lesson.

Also remember the boomerang principle: if you want to influence other people, help them look for the good when things are going wrong. When somebody is having a problem, say, "You know, there's something good in everything that happens. I wonder what it could be here." Help them focus their minds on finding something good. When a person has a reversal or a setback, say, "There's one or more lessons in every problem. I wonder what it could be here." Help them identify the lessons. In both cases, you help these people get back in touch with reality, put their dimmer switches on full, become positive and creative, and elicit all the benefits contained in those difficulties. Simultaneously, you make yourself a more positive and constructive person.

4. Feeding your mind with positive, uplifting material—books, audios, courses, positive conversations, seminars and conferences given by people who are positive and constructive—has an inordinate influence on your mind. It makes you happier and more positive, gives you more energy, and motivates you to do more, as opposed to sitting and watching all the terrible things online or on television.

You Are Responsible

There's a simple antidote to dealing with fear, doubt, and worry and to becoming more optimistic: all negativity ultimately comes down to blame. You can only be negative about a situation if you are blaming someone else. You can only be angry if you're blaming someone else. You can only be resentful if you're blaming someone else. When you stop blaming, your negative emotion stops at the same time.

The way to cancel negative emotions is to say the words *I am responsible* over and over again. Whenever you say the words *I am responsible*, you cancel the negative emotion, because you cannot accept responsibility and be negative simultaneously.

The words *I am responsible* are extremely powerful. I spent four thousand hours and three years of study in this area of psychology, because I was so overwhelmed with the importance of this concept. All happiness and success in life come from positive emotions. In the absence of positive emotions, negative emotions emerge automatically. But you can cancel negative emotions just by saying, *I am responsible. I'm not going to blame someone else. I am not a victim. Things went wrong. I'm not going to complain, criticize, whine, or moan. No. I am responsible.*

When you say the words *I am responsible*, you feel like a power in your own life. You take control over what's happening to you, your mind goes calm, and you have clear ideas about what to do next.

All leaders are highly self-responsible people. Every book on success, whether it's Jack Canfield's *Success Principles* or Stephen Covey's *Seven Habits of Highly Successful People*, begins with, "Take charge; take responsibility; stop making excuses. Decide what you want, and go for it."

Responsibility is the dividing line between childhood and adulthood. When you're a child, you blame your problems on your parents, on what they did or didn't do. But when you become an adult, as the Bible says, you "put away childish things" (1 Corinthians 13:11). When you become an adult, you step across that line, and you say, "I am an adult. I am responsible for what happens to me from now on." From then on, your life will be different.

If you love and respect the people around you, encourage them to accept responsibility as well. In my company, I say, "Everybody here is the president of their own personal services corporation. You are responsible. If something goes wrong, you're responsible for solving it." People come into my office and say, "I've got a problem, but I'm the president of my own company. Here's what I propose we do."

I tell my children the same thing: always accept responsibility. If they come in and something's gone wrong, I ask, "What's up?" They say, "I have this problem, I have this difficulty, but I am responsible, and this is what I've learned."

From an early age, my children have been self-responsible and lesson learning. As they've gotten older, their confidence and self-esteem have gone up. They know they can handle any situation because they take responsibility and look for the lesson, and so can you.

Negative emotions make you feel bad and see yourself as a victim. Accepting responsibility makes you feel powerful and in control of yourself and your life. There's a direct relationship between accepting responsibility and a sense of control. As I've already pointed out, there's also a direct relationship between having a sense of control and positive emotions. You feel great about yourself to the degree to which you feel you're in control of your life. When you accept responsibility, you take complete control. When you take complete control, you feel happy.

Positive affirmations—positive statements that you make to yourself with emotion—are the way to take complete control over your emotions and program yourself for success in the future.

Positive affirmations enable you to unlock your potential at a higher level than you ever thought possible. The most powerful confidence building statements are *I like myself. I like myself. I am responsible. I can do it.*

Often when you get up in the morning, you will not say, "Good morning, God"; you'll say, "Good God, it's morning." You can get yourself cranked up by immediately starting to say, *I like myself. I love my work. I like myself. I love my work.* Pretty soon you'll start to feel good; you'll feel happy. Your brain releases endorphins, which are nature's happy drug. Your liver releases glycogen, which is a form of energy, and you feel pumped and ready to go.

Five Ways to a Positive Attitude

There are five ways to build greater optimism, self-confidence, and a positive mental attitude:

1. Create an exciting vision of your ideal future, as if you had no limitations. The very act of thinking about an exciting future raises your self-esteem and improves your self-image. Just imagining a wonderful life will motivate you and make you happy. Imagine yourself, visualize yourself, earning twice as much as you're earn-

ing today. Then visualize yourself earning three times as much, five times as much, and ten times as much.

Visualize yourself living a wonderful life in every area. Get magazines that wealthy people read—like *The Robb Report* or *Architectural Digest*—that show beautiful homes, pictures, yachts, planes, watches, clothes, and resorts. Read those magazines and say, *I can do this; I'm going to do that.*

Put yourself into the pictures in the ads. Imagine you could live in a house like this, you could enjoy vacations like this, you could take yacht cruises like this, you could wear clothes like this. The more you flood your mind with these pictures, the more your superconscious mind will work to find ways to make them a reality.

2. Create written goals and plans for your future, and work on them every day. As inspirational speaker Earl Nightingale said, "Happiness is the progressive realization of a worthy ideal." When you feel yourself moving forward toward something that's important to you, you feel happy, you feel powerful, you feel in control of your life. It's not reaching the destination; it's the forward motion that gives you the feeling of positive motivation.

Write down your goals by using the three P's: *positive*, *personal*, *present*. First, use the present tense. Your subconscious mind cannot deal with any other tense but the present. Write down your goal as if the goal has already been achieved. For example, say, "I earn X number of dollars each year." "I weigh X number of pounds as my permanent weight." Say it as though it's already a fact.

This sets up a dynamic within your subconscious and superconscious mind that starts working twenty-four hours a day to make your new command your reality.

Second, always state your goals in positive terms. Your subconscious mind cannot accept a negative command. It cannot accept, "Lose weight." Instead say, "I weigh X number of pounds." Instead of saying, "Quit smoking," say, "I am a nonsmoker."

Third, use the first person. Use the word *I* plus an action verb. You are the only person in the universe who can use the word *I* with regard to yourself. Whenever you use the word *I*, your subconscious mind recognizes this as a command coming from the head office: *I* earn, *I* sell, *I* achieve, *I* run, *I* accomplish. Whenever you use *I* plus an action verb, it has a powerful impact on changing your behavior.

Another way to make your goals work for you is to write and rewrite them every morning in the PPP form—*positive*, *personal*, *present*—in a spiral notebook. Or you can write each goal in big letters on a three by five index card and reread them regularly throughout the day. Read the card, close your eyes, and imagine the goal as a reality. Carry these cards around with you. Whenever you have a spare moment, pull them out and read the goals to yourself. Each time you read the goal, your subconscious mind photographs the command, and it goes deeper into your subconscious mind.

Finally, when you are writing and rewriting your goals, create the feeling within yourself that would accompany the realized goals. If you would feel proud, then imagine yourself feeling proud. If you would feel confident, liked, loved, lovable— whatever it happens to be—if you can connect the emotion with the goal, the two together have an even greater impact on your subconscious and superconscious minds, and the results come faster into your life.

3. Resolve to be the best at your job. Resolve to join the top 10 percent. Set it as a goal. You'll never become a member of the top 10 percent unless you set it as a goal. When I talk to people, I ask, "How many people here have decided to be mediocre in their careers?" Nobody raises their hand. I say, "Do you know that you have an automatic default mechanism on your brain, and that if you do not decide to be excellent, you default to mediocrity?"

   People are shocked. They say, "I want to be good at my job." I say, "Yes, but have you *decided* to be good? Have you written it down? Have you set it as a goal? Do you work on it every single day? Do you constantly evaluate yourself and get feedback from others so you know how well you're doing?" "No, I don't do that, but I want to be good at what I do."

   It's not enough. You've got to be crystal clear about getting into the top 10 percent, and you have to work at it relentlessly until you do.

   Here's the good news. Every step you take toward becoming better in your field raises your self-esteem and self-confidence, unlocks ideas and energy for goal attainment, motivates you, and drives you forward to earn respect, esteem, and praise from the people around you. The payoff is the journey as much as reaching the destination.

Here's a question: what one skill, if you were absolutely excellent at it, would most help you to join the top 10 percent in your field? Whatever that skill is, write it down. Make a list of everything you could do to develop this skill and work on it every day.

Remember, the flip side of self-esteem is self-efficacy. When you commit to excellence, to becoming very good at what you do, you like yourself more, and you perform better in every area.

4. Deal effectively with problems and obstacles. Life is an unending series of problems, like the waves coming in from the ocean. As Henry Kissinger said, "All you get for solving problems is the authority to solve even bigger problems." Your ability to deal effectively with your problems is the key to personal power, self-esteem, and self-confidence. No matter what happens, always start off by saying, *I am responsible.* Take control, then focus on the solution rather than the problem. Think about what can be done rather than what happened. Think positively about actions that you can take immediately to resolve the situation. There seems to be a direct relationship between positive, constructive action and self-confidence.

5. Get busy working on your goals all day long. Decide today to go on a twenty-one-day positive mental attitude diet. It takes about twenty-one days to develop a new habit of medium complexity. With a twenty-one-day positive mental attitude diet, you take complete control over your present and your future. For twenty-one days, you resolve to think and talk about what you want. Say, "OK, after twenty-one days, I can go back, but for these days, I'm only going to think about what I want. I'm only going to think about actions I can take to achieve what I want." Meanwhile, you refuse to criticize, complain, or blame others for anything; you just refuse.

   If you carry out these steps, in twenty-one days you will have reprogrammed yourself for life. You will have laid down a whole new series of neural tracks in your brain that cause you to easily and automatically think positively most of the time. As the German poet and philosopher Goethe said, "Everything is hard before it's easy."

Is it easy to become a positive, forward-focused, high-energy person? No, but it's learnable through practice and repetition. Your new positive habits of thinking and acting will soon become automatic and easy. You'll get up in the morning, and you'll already like yourself and love your work. You'll go through the day knowing, "I can do it. I can do anything I put my mind to." Whenever you have problems, you'll say, "I am responsible. I'm in charge of my life." You'll become a completely positive person. You will take complete control over your mind and your emotions.

4

How to Influence Others

The first, foundational steps of the Phoenix Transformation have to do with you: harnessing the power of your mind, determining what you want in life, and directing your intention accordingly. Now it's time to turn to another major element in your success: other people.

Approximately 85 percent of your success will be determined by your ability to communicate effectively with others. Almost everything you accomplish will be associated with other people in some way. People account for 85 percent of your happiness and your results. Therefore the quality of your communications determines the quality of your relationships of all kinds, as well as the quality of your life. The good news is that communicating is a skill that you can learn with practice.

Five Goals for Interactions

Here are the five most important goals to accomplish in your interactions with others:

1. You want people to like and respect you in order to reinforce and validate your self-image. How we think and feel about ourselves is strongly affected by how other people think and feel about us, and by how we think other people think and feel about us. If we think people like us and respect us, we like and respect ourselves more, we do a better job, we get better results, and we get along better with others.

2. In order to build your self-esteem and feelings of worthiness, you want people to feel that you are valuable and important. Our self-esteem is fragile, like a piece of Venetian glass. People can raise or lower our self-esteem by the things that they do or don't do, say or don't say. We want people to validate our self-esteem. We want people to feel that we're valuable.

3. We want to be able to persuade people to our point of view so that we can sell our products, services, and ideas to others.

   Do you know that your ability to persuade others is the mark of the integration of your personality? People with great personalities are persuasive. People with poor personalities are not.

If your job is in sales or business, your ability to persuade others is crucial. It's absolutely essential for your success for banks to lend you money, for customers to buy your product, for suppliers to give you credit.

4. You want to get people to change their minds and to cooperate with you in achieving your goals.

5. You want to be personally powerful and effective in all your relationships in your personal and business life.

These are also the keys to success in life, love, and leadership.

Emotional Intelligence

In 1995, the psychologist Daniel Goleman published the breakthrough best seller *Emotional Intelligence.* In it, he argued that EQ, or emotional quotient—that is, your emotional intelligence—is more important than IQ, or intelligence quotient. He concluded that your ability to persuade others is the highest form of emotional intelligence that you can develop and the true measure of how effective you are as a person.

How, then, do you get your ideas across to others, get people to cooperate with you, and develop the abilities to communicate, influence, and persuade others? The first thing to understand is that people do things for their reasons, not yours. To communicate and persuade effectively, you must find out what their own motives are.

The next key is to get out of yourself and get into the mind, heart, and situation of the other person. Focus on that person's needs and desires rather than your own. My friend Ed Foreman used to say, "If you can see Joe Jones through Joe Jones' eyes, you can sell Joe Jones what Joe Jones buys." Constantly try to see the situation through the eyes of the other person.

Before going into a major sale or negotiation, I used to sit down and write a list of all the things that the other person wanted and needed to accomplish in this negotiation. Once I had done that, I would come back and ask how I could structure my offer or presentation so that it was in harmony with those needs. Every time I did this, I got fabulous results, without exception. Start off by thinking about the other person, and you'll be amazed at how much better a communicator you are.

The third way to persuade others is remember that you can only do so if they believe that you can do something for them or to them, or if they believe that you can stop something from being done to or for them. In other words, people are pretty selfish. They look at you and say, "What can this person do to or for me?" or "What can this person stop from being done to or for me?"

People are motivated by two major factors. First is the desire for gain. Everybody wants more. For six thousand years of recorded history, going back to the earliest markets in ancient Sumeria, customers have only bought one thing—improvement. They buy because they feel they will be better off after buying than they were before. They desire physical, material, financial, emotional gain—pride, security, peace of mind, riches, value, growth, profits.

The second motivation is the fear of loss. This can also be physical loss or danger, insecurity, material or financial loss, emotional loss, loss of love, affection, respect, and so on. Those two forces compete back and forth in the mind of each person you speak to. In both cases your job is to persuade them that they will be better off by cooperating with you than otherwise.

Here's a rule: the fear of loss is 2.5 times more powerful than the desire for gain in motivating human behavior. If you're going to present a product or a service, show how the prospect will benefit them if they buy, but also show the detriments or loss if they don't. Trigger both motivations: desire for gain and fear of loss.

Everything is perception. How people perceive you—as being able to help them or hurt them in some way—largely determines how they react to you. You could be talking to someone and you could have the feeling that this person can do nothing to help you or hurt you at all. They are irrelevant. Then someone comes along says, "Oh, by the way, have you met this person? This person is potentially a million-dollar customer for your product, and he's in the market right now and is in a hurry to make a purchase." Suddenly your entire perception of this person transforms.

All of human behavior is based on the expediency factor, which means that people always strive to get the things they want the fastest and easiest way possible, with little immediate concern for the long-term consequences of their actions. In other words, people are lazy, greedy, and impatient. They want it, and they want it now. Sometimes they want it yesterday, and they don't really care about the long-term ramifications. One of the hardest of all things for parents to develop in their children is long-term perspective: thinking over the long term about the things that they're doing in the present. People say, "I want a piece of cheesecake," but they don't think about how long it will take to work off that piece of cheesecake if they have to exercise.

The great motivating factor is that people seek fast, easy, quick, and expedient ways to get what they want. Your job is to make your idea or proposal appear to be the most expedient way for the other person to achieve their personal and business goals. If you cannot show the person that the fastest and easiest way to get where they want is to do what you want them to do, then you can't possibly expect them to accept your recommendation.

Four Keys to Persuasion

There are four keys to persuasion. We call these the four Ps. The first is *personal power.* The more people see you as having power over people, money, or resources, the more open they are to being persuaded by you. If the president of the United States walked up to you and demanded that you do something, you'd be much more influenced by it than if a waiter came up and asked you the same thing, because we perceive the president's personal power over people, money, and resources.

The second key to persuasion is *positioning*—how people think and talk about you, your reputation among the people you are trying to persuade. When you have a tremendous reputation for being competent, for being a good person, for being honest, for being wealthy, or for being an expert in your field, you have a greater influence over other people.

The third area of persuasion is *performance*—your ability and competence in your field. A reputation for expertise and knowledge enables you to persuade other people to your point of view far more easily than if they didn't feel that you knew any more than they did.

Number four is *politeness*: the use of kindness, courtesy, and respect in all your dealings with others. The deepest need that each person has is for a feeling of importance and value. When you satisfy this deep craving, people become much more open to your persuasion and to your efforts to communicate.

The most powerful influence factor in psychology is liking. The more people like you, the more open they are to being persuaded and influenced by you. This is the key to effective communication.

Making People Feel Important

As I've said, the simplest of all communication tools is to make people feel important. There are five ways to make people feel important. We call them the five A's.

The first A is *acceptance*. The practice of acceptance satisfies a deep, subconscious need. Each person needs to feel accepted by others around them—in their work environment, in their home environment, by people they meet. They watch for it. Whenever two people meet, the first thing that is established is a level of acceptance of some kind.

The way you express acceptance of other people is simple: you smile and act as if you're happy to see them. When I go into my office after being away for a week or two, the first thing I do is go from person to person, like a hummingbird going from flower to flower. I smile at each person and say, "How are you? It's nice to see you; it's nice to be back." I go from person to person, acknowledge them, and tell them that they're important parts of our company. You can do the same thing.

By the way, each time you see a member of your family, your spouse or your child, smile: "Wow, it's you!" as though you're happy to see them again. This has an enormously positive impact on how important they feel and how open they are to your influence.

The second A is *appreciation*. Expressing appreciation is very simple: just say thank you for everything that people do for you, large and small. Say thank you all the time. When a waiter brings you a glass of water, say thank you. When somebody steps aside for you, say thank you. When somebody types a letter for you or brings you in to see customers, say thank you.

The more you say thank you, the more you cause the other person's self-esteem to go up. They feel more valuable and important. They like themselves better. They beam, and they like you better as well. You cannot say thank you too often.

A friend of mine wrote to me saying he was traveling to the Far East. Since I've traveled in many countries all over the world, he wondered if I could give him some advice on how to get along well. I said, "Remember, everybody you're dealing with earns less, and usually far less, than you could ever imagine. They don't have anything going for them except their own personal value. If you acknowledge that, you'll have a great trip. The way you do that is to learn how to say *please* and *thank you* in their language. Whenever you meet people, smile and say *please* and *thank you*. Whatever they do for you, express gratitude, and you will have a wonderful trip."

My friend wrote back to me two months later, saying it was the best advice he had ever gotten his whole life. He could not believe it. Everywhere he went, even when people were standoffish or reserved, when he said *please* and *thank you* and smiled, he got everything he wanted. He got upgraded to better rooms, and he got better tables in restaurants—all by just making other people feel important.

The third A is *admiration*: you express sincere compliments for the traits, accomplishments, and possessions of other people. Everybody likes compliments. They make people feel valuable and important.

People put a lot of emotional investment into different factors of their life. If a person is punctual, say, "You know, you're the most punctual person in this whole company." If a person is persistent, say, "Boy, you're sure persistent; you never give up." People are very proud of their character traits, because it's taken them a long time to develop them. If a person has accomplished something, graduated from a college, completed a degree, or gotten a certification, admire that and say, "Wow, that's really great. You must be really proud of that. That must have taken a lot of work." People who have put many hours into those accomplishments feel really happy about themselves.

Admire their possessions, particularly clothing. When you compliment a person on their hair or clothing—a man on his shirt or shoes, a woman on her dress, handbag, or hairstyle—they beam. They feel valuable, their self-esteem goes up, they like themselves more, and they feel happier in your presence. All it takes is a couple of seconds for you to acknowledge and point out something that's worth a compliment.

Number four is *approval*. You express approval by giving praise for both small and large accomplishments. Self-esteem is the degree to which a person feels praise-worthy. When you praise a person for doing a good job, for a result, praise for anything that they've put effort into, their self-esteem surges, and they feel really happy about themselves.

The key point is to be specific with your praise, and be immediate. If a secretary types a letter for you, don't say, "You're a great secretary." Say, "That is a really excellent letter," and tell her immediately after it is typed. Give an immediate compliment, because the more closely the compliment follows after the event, the more likely the person is to follow up and repeat that behavior.

Praise that is delayed or deferred has little effect on the emotions or behavior of the other person. If you wait for a week or a month to praise the person, it's too late. They'll have forgotten all about the antecedents, and they'll just roll their eyes. Praise immediately. I phone people, I email people, I text people to praise them when I hear that they've done something good.

Finally, number five is *attention*, which is listening to people when they talk. This is powerful. When you listen to people, they feel good about themselves. They feel valuable and important, and like flowers, they will open up to be influenced and persuaded by you.

Each of these behaviors raises the self-esteem of the other person. It makes them more open to your ideas and more desirous of helping you achieve your goals.

The White Magic of Listening

In fact, effective listening is the key to leadership, persuasion, and good communications. It is so powerful that it's often called white magic. There are four keys to being a great listener:

1. Listen attentively, lean forward, and don't interrupt. When you listen attentively, you raise the other person's self-esteem and make them feel important, happy, and valuable. Their brain releases endorphins, which makes them feel happy about being in your presence. Effective listening with no attempt to interrupt is very powerful.

   When you listen to another person, imagine that your eyes are sunlamps and you want to give the other person's face a tan. The more intensely you listen, the more powerful the sunlamps of your eyes are and the better tan you give. You also want to give the face of the other person an overall tan. Keep flicking your eyes up and down, look at the person's mouth and eyes, nod, and smile. This has an enormous impact on causing them to feel good about themselves and liking you.

2. Pause before replying. In other words, when a person stops to take a breath, don't jump in with your two cents' worth; allow silence in the conversation.

   This benefits you in three ways. First of all, you avoid the risk of interrupting if the person is just reorganizing their thoughts. Second, it allows you to hear at a deeper level. When you pause and listen, you actually hear and understand what the person is saying far better than if you just jump in. The third benefit is that pausing tells the person that you consider his or her words to be important, which means, by extension, that you consider him or her to be important as well.

3. Question for clarification. Never assume that you know what the other person meant by what he or she said. Instead, if there's any question at all, say, "How do you mean exactly?" Whenever you ask that question, the other person will expand on what they just said. Then you pause and say, "Well, how do you mean?" They'll expand again. Sometimes you can go through an entire conversation just by repeating this one question.

   Another question you can ask: "Then what did you do?" If they're telling you something has happened and they pause to see if you're really interested, say, "Then what did you do?" Listen attentively to the answers.

The third question is, "How did you feel about that?" People will always answer a feeling question. When you ask, how do you feel today? people always give you an answer. So you can ask, how do you feel about that deal? How do you feel about your new neighborhood? People will always answer a feeling question, which gives you a chance to nod and listen.

The person who asks questions has control over the person who's answering the questions. The more questions you ask, the more control you have in the conversation.

4. Feed back what you've heard, and paraphrase it in your own words. This is the acid test of listening. When a person finishes speaking, say, "Let me make sure I understand what you're saying," or, "So what you're saying is this . . ." You rephrase their remarks until they say, "Yes, that's it. That's my concern. That's what I was saying."

   This proves to the other person that you were truly listening. You weren't like one of those little dogs with its head bobbing in the back of a car. You were genuinely listening to what they said. It proves to the other person that you care about them and what they say.

Credibility

The most important word in persuasion, influence, and communicating with power is *credibility*. How much does a person like you, trust you, and believe in what you say? It's determined by your credibility. The rule with regard to credibility is that everything counts. Everything helps or hurts; everything adds up or takes away from your credibility. Nothing is overlooked or ignored.

The key to being trusted is to be trustworthy. Keep your promises. Do what you say you will do. Be punctual for every meeting. Develop a reputation for honesty and dependability. People will buy more from, and pay more to, a company that is reliable than to one that offers a better and cheaper product or service but is not reliable.

Dress for Success

To communicate effectively with others, you must look the part as well. People are 95 percent visual in their thinking. They think about you in pictures. It only takes four seconds to make the first impression. When you meet a person the first time, they take one glance at you, like a snapshot. They blink, and they've made their first impression of you. It takes only thirty seconds to finalize the person's impression of you.

In other words, once the person has made their first impression, they begin watching, and their mind begins to set like fast-drying concrete. If you do not change this first impression within the next thirty seconds, the mind will set. After this impression is solidified, the person seeks reasons to justify and validate it. This is called *selective perception*. They look for information to validate what they've already decided while simultaneously rejecting all contradictory information.

Dress for success, because your clothes are 95 percent of your first impression on others. Even on a hot day, your clothes cover 95 percent of your body.

When I was a young salesman, I bought a cheap suit that fit me poorly, I got a tie, and I put them together. I did not come from a family where anybody ever wore ties, so I didn't know anything about it.

One day an older salesman took me aside and said, "Could I give you a little feedback on your dress?" He was very tentative about it, because most people are really sensitive about their dress and grooming. I said, "Absolutely. Do you see anything I could improve?" He said, "Yes, let me tell you a little bit about proper dress in business." He began talking about the way a suit hangs, the way it's cut, the seams, how a tie goes with a suit and a shirt, the length of the trousers, the color of socks and shoes. I couldn't believe that there was so much to it. He then introduced me to a tailor (although not an expensive one), who made me a suit. In one study described in *Psychology Today*, people who were shown three-second images of men wearing a bespoke (custom-tailored) suit described them as "more confident, successful, flexible," and higher earners than men in a suit bought off the rack.

The difference between a suit that fit me and a suit that I bought off the rack was almost miraculous. After that, I went out and I bought book after book on how to dress properly. I got advice from the best people on the subject. Now when I do a seminar, people will come up to me and say, "You know, I'm an image consultant, I charge $500 or $1,000 a day to advise people on proper dress, and you are dressed impeccably." It makes a tremendous impression for you to have your plumage in a way that impresses other people.

Attire is also important for women in the professional world—so much so that an international nonprofit organization, Dress for Success (named after a celebrated best seller by John Molloy), has been formed to empower women "to achieve economic independence by providing a network of support, professional attire and the development tools to help them thrive in work and in life."

Get and read books and articles on how to dress successfully in your business or occupation. Some clothes, colors, and combinations immediately cause people to stand up and salute. Others cause people to downgrade you and look upon you with suspicion.

Look at the most successful and respected people around you. Make them your role models. Copy their ways of dress and grooming. Because I wanted to be successful in business, I would read business magazines. I would also read the pages that show photographs of people who have just been appointed to more senior positions. Look at the way they're dressed. In every case, male and female, they look great.

These rapidly changing times are transforming dress standards as well. Over recent decades, many professions have been moving away from the once-standard suit and tie (for men) to "business casual." For men, this generally means dress slacks or chinos, dress shoes (not sneakers), collared shirts (without neckties), and sports jackets. For women, the mode is generally a blouse, a skirt or dress slacks, and shoes with appropriate heels or flats. Of course, styles vary wildly between industries and professions, so you will need to observe the people you look up to and take hints from the way they dress.

Always dress for the job that you want in the future. Dress so that your boss would be proud to introduce you to customers or somebody visiting your company. Always dress ahead of where you are in life. When you look at people you admire, make them your role models: copy their ways of dress, copy their ways of grooming. Birds of a feather flock together. People promote people who look like them.

If you're going to sell something to someone, you're giving them advice. Dress the way the people who give them advice would dress—their bankers, lawyers, accountants. Preparation is a powerful way to communicate and build credibility.

Preparation and Reliability

Before every meeting, do your homework. People know immediately when you are well prepared for a meeting. Your credibility goes straight up when you walk in and say, "Thank you very much for your time. I took a little bit of time to go on the Internet and look at your site. I was quite amazed to see that you've been in business for twelve years, you have 127 people in your company, and you're the top distributor of this particular product or service in this market. How did you accomplish that?"

Your credibility goes straight through the roof: "What? You've done some research, you've checked us out, you've learned something about us before you came here?" That's one of the most powerful things you can do in selling and persuasion.

People also know immediately when you're unprepared for a meeting. When you come in and say, "What do you do here anyway? How long have you been in business? What does this company do?" your credibility goes straight through the floor. (I used to say these things when I was younger.)

By the way, the rule with regard to preparation is, never ask a question of a person in an organization if you can easily find the answer somewhere else. Dale Carnegie, author of *The Power of Positive Thinking*, used to say that you have to earn the right to call on a customer; you earn that right by doing your homework before you get there.

To influence people in business, always refer back to the expediency principle. In business especially, people buy or decline to buy on the basis of their conclusion that your offering is the fastest and best way to get what they want right now, or not.

Liking is the most important factor in communicating effectively in business. The more people like you, the more open they are to buying from you. Credibility and trust are the most powerful reasons for being persuaded by another person. Always think of how you could be more credible and more trustworthy.

Someone once said that the most important ability in business is dependability. Social proof is the key to influencing people. Refer to others who have accepted your idea or product and who are happy with it.

People are inordinately influenced in their decisions by what are called *similar others*: people like them. When you call on a doctor as a salesperson, you say, "Many other doctors are now using this product with great results." That immediately raises your credibility and opens the doctor up to learning more about your offering. If you're talking to a truck driver, you say that a lot of truck drivers are now using this product for this reason. If you're talking to a real estate agent, you say that top real estate agents use this all the time.

In other words, whenever you're talking to somebody, refer to someone else in their field who is also using your product. Use letters from these people, use lists of names from people in similar fields, and use photographs of people employing your product or service in a similar field.

You build buying desire by focusing on the benefits and by continually answering the question, "What's in it for me?" This is the one question that you have to answer over and over again. Always explain the different ways that the person will be better off using your product or service. Always show how their life or work will improve when they accept your advice.

Gender Differences

There are several differences between men and women in communicating, persuading, and influencing. Although there are exceptions in every case, basically, men are direct, and women are indirect. Men are like javelins, and women are like boxers: they circle around the subject. Men want recommendation; women prefer to choose from a selection of available items.

In sales, if you're talking to a man, you say, "Here are the three options, and what I recommend for you, based on what you've said, is this, for these reasons." With a woman, you say, "Here are the three options. Here are the pros and cons; which choice do you prefer?" Women like to choose; men like a recommendation.

Another difference in communications between men and women is that men use words as tools to do a job: they use as few tools as they need to. Women use words to connect, nurture, and build relationships. Men like to make quick practical decisions. Women prefer to listen to their emotions and take more time in making decisions. Men are motivated by success, status, power, results, and achievement. Women are more concerned with family, children, friends, and relationships.

Men like to talk about sports, business, and politics. Women prefer to talk about people, relationships, and emotions. If you ever go to a social function where there are two or three couples, you'll find that the men cluster and begin to talk about sports, business, and politics. The women cluster and begin to talk about people, family, relationships, and emotions. It's automatic.

Whenever I go out for dinner with, say, three couples, I always put the three women together and the three men together. People say, "What about the boy, girl, boy, girl setup?" I say, "You spend lots of time with the other person. Let's put the women together, because they will instantly start talking about things that are of interest to women.

The men will immediately start talking about things that are of interest to men, and both groups will have a great time."

Another interesting point: men can only focus on one thing at a time. Women can talk, listen, interact, and do other things simultaneously.

To get along better with women, men need to ask more questions, listen more attentively, and offer fewer suggestions or solutions. A woman may bring a problem to a man, saying, "I have this problem at work, and this is what has happened. What do you think?" In fact, she's already decided what she's going to do.

She's only asking to start a conversation, because women like to talk to the men in their lives. They use this kind of situation as an opportunity to start the engine and get the conversation going. The last thing they want is a solution.

Men will reply by giving a specific solution and go back to watching television. That's not what the woman wants. She wants to talk: "Oh, how did it happen? What do you think you should do?" A woman might ask a question like, "Should I wear these earrings or those? Which do you think goes best with that dress? Which to wear—these shoes or those shoes? Which do you like better?" If you say, "I like the brown ones," she'll say, "I think I'll wear the beige ones." She's pretty much decided what she's going to wear, so throw the question back to her; she just wants to talk. Ask questions and ask for her opinion rather than offering suggestions or solutions.

To get along better with men, women need to be more direct, to be clear about what they want, and to ask for help or involvement. Although women can read minds, men cannot. Every man has had an experience where he'll call home and say, "Hello." The woman will ask, "What's wrong? Is it your boss? Is it what happened this morning?" She'll put it all together with hello. It's like the famous line from the movie *Jerry Maguire*, where the lead female character says, "You had me at hello." She knew everything, just from hello. Women are like that.

One problem, by the way, that arises with men and women is that when women interact with other women, they can read one another's minds and know what they're thinking and feeling. They're very sensitive to it, and they respond appropriately. Women expect men to be the same way. But we aren't, because we're not constructed that way. Women sometimes become resentful. They say, "Why not? It's because he's not trying." No: it's because he's not capable of it. This is very important to understand.

Men do not think a great deal about relationships or communications. Women think a lot about relationships and communications. It's a fundamental difference between the two. Men have very simple inner lives; women have very complex inner lives. If you take a man and a woman sitting on a couch watching television, the man's brain will shut down to about 20 percent of capacity, like the lights of an office building at night. If you put an EEG on a woman's head while she's watching the same program, 80 percent of her brain will be fully activated. It'll be going off and on. She'll be thinking about what she's watching, how the plot is developing, but she'll also be thinking about what she did earlier in the day, what she's going to do tomorrow, and so on.

Comedian Jerry Seinfeld was once asked, "What do men think about?" His answer was, "Not much. They just sit there, and they don't think about much."

A woman comes along and says, "What are you thinking?" The man believes he's got to say something, although he wasn't thinking anything at all. Worst of all is when a woman comes to a man saying, "What are you feeling?" or, "How do you feel?" The man's not feeling anything; he's just sitting there. It's really important that men and women understand the fundamental differences in the ways they communicate.

Resolve today to become an expert in communicating with power. Read books on the subject, attend courses on effective communication, listen to audio programs, and most of all, practice, practice, practice.

5

Goals: The Building Blocks

As we've already seen, one of the basic keys to success is knowing what you want and committing yourself to getting it. In order to keep yourself on track, you also have to know how to set, and commit yourself to, specific goals.

Once upon a time, several very successful people got together, and they were talking about what they'd accomplished and why. One of them spoke up and said, "You know what success is?" Everyone else became quiet and listened. He went on: "Success is goals; all else is commentary."

This is one of the great truths in life: *success is goals, and all else is commentary.* This is the great discovery throughout all of human history. Your life only begins to become a great life when you clearly identify what you want, plan to achieve it, and work on that plan every single day.

Napoleon Hill once said, "The primary reason for failure is that people do not develop new plans to replace those plans that didn't work." I've found that when you start off on a new goal or course of action, most things won't work, at least not the first time. Many people try something once and then quit. Successful people try and try again: they make new plans, make different plans, try something different. They keep on going.

Over the years, I've done thousands of radio and television interviews, and they always ask me, "What was the turning point for you? What was the Saul on the road to Damascus experience that took you from rags to riches, that got you out of the ditch of life?"

I used to get irritated when I heard that, because it assumes that there's just one quick trick that makes a person successful, so I would dance around the question. Then one day I thought, "There *were* turning points in my life." I realized that there were three. I find that they are the three turning points for everybody.

First, I discovered that I was responsible for my life and for everything that happened to me. I learned that this life is not a rehearsal for something else. This is the real thing.

This was a real shock to me. Up to that time, I blamed my background, my parents, and things that had happened to me. Suddenly, like a flashbulb in the face, I realized I was responsible, and if anything was going to change in my life, I was going to have to change it myself.

Every study of successful people shows that their starting point is the acceptance of personal responsibility.

Before that, nothing happens. After you accept complete responsibility, your whole life begins to change.

The second turning point for me, which came when I was about twenty-four years old, was my discovery of goals. Without really knowing what I was doing, I sat down and made a list of ten things I wanted to accomplish in the foreseeable future. I promptly lost the list. But thirty days later, my whole life had changed. Almost every goal in my list had already been achieved or partially achieved.

The third turning point in my life came when I discovered that you can learn anything you need to learn in order to accomplish any goal you can set for yourself. No one is smarter than you, and no one is better than you. All business skills, sales skills, and moneymaking skills are learnable.

Everyone who is good in any area today was once poor in that area. The top people in every field were at one time not even in that field and didn't even know that it existed. What hundreds of thousands, or millions, of other people have done in achieving success you can do as well.

Ten Steps in Goal Setting

I want to walk you through some of the critical steps of the goal setting process.

1. Decide exactly what you want in every key area of your life. You do this by starting off idealizing. Idealizing is a special technique used by top people all over the world and throughout history. Imagine that there are no lim-

itations on what you can be, or have, or do. Imagine that you have all the time, all the money, all the friends, all the contacts, all the education, all the experience that you need to accomplish any goal you can set for yourself.

Imagine that you could wave a magic wand and make your life perfect in each of the four key areas of life. If your life was perfect in each of these areas, what would it look like?

The first area is income. How much do you want to earn this year, next year, and five years from today? Wave a magic wand, and imagine that you have no limits.

The second area has to do with your family. What kind of lifestyle do you want to create for yourself and your family? What kind of a home do you want to live in? What kind of vacations do you want to take? What do you want to accomplish for members of your family? Just imagine you have no limits, and you could design your perfect lifestyle.

The third area has to do with your health. How would your health be different if it was perfect in every way? How much would you weigh? How fit would you be? What time would you get up in the morning? What kind of foods would you eat? How would you feel if you had perfect health? Just imagine you have no limits.

The fourth area has to do with your net worth. How much do you want to save and accumulate in the course of your working lifetime? What is your long-term financial goal?

Remember, you can't hit a target that you can't see. The more clarity you have about your financial goals, the more likely you are to make the right decisions on the way to reaching them.

Here's a technique you can use. I call it the three-goal method. Write down your three most important goals in life right now. Take thirty seconds, and write them as fast as you can—bang, bang, bang.

Your answers are probably an accurate picture of what you really want in life. We have found that if you have only thirty seconds to write your three goals, your answers will be as accurate as if you had thirty minutes or three hours. Somehow your superconscious and subconscious mind go into overdrive and pop, pop, pop—there are your three major goals.

2. Write your goals down. They must be in writing, and they must be clear, specific, detailed, and measurable. You must write out your goals as if you were placing an order to be manufactured in a factory at a great distance. Make your description clear and detailed in every sense.

   Only 3 percent of adults have written goals. Not only do these people earn ten times as much as the average person, but everyone else works for them. There are many cases where people come to our country with no knowledge of anybody, no context, no language skills, and ten years later, they have hundreds of people working for them, and they're wealthy. Why? It's because they had goals; they were clear about what they wanted.

3. Set deadlines. Your subconscious mind uses deadlines to drive you, consciously and unconsciously, toward achieving your goal on schedule. If it is big enough, set sub-deadlines. For example, if you want to achieve financial independence, you may set a ten- or twenty-year goal. Then break it down year by year so that you know how much you have to save and invest each year.

   If for some reason you don't achieve your goal by the deadline, simply set a new deadline. There are no unrealistic goals, only unrealistic deadlines. Sometimes you can have a logical, realistic goal, and situations, circumstances, and financial conditions will change dramatically, so you'll have to set a new deadline.

4. Identify the obstacles that you will have to overcome to achieve your goal. You identify them by asking why you aren't already at your goal.

   There's a principle called the *principle of constraints*. It's one of the best thinking tools I've ever learned. It says that there's always one limiting factor or constraint—sometimes we call it a bottleneck—that sets the speed at which you achieve your goal. What is it for you? What is your constraint? What's holding you back? The 80–20 rule applies to constraints. It says that fully 80 percent of the reasons that are holding you back from achieving your goal are inside yourself. They are usually the lack of a skill, a quality, or a body of knowledge. Only 20 percent of the reasons you are not achieving your goal are on the outside. Always start with yourself and ask, what is it in me that is holding me back?

5. Determine the knowledge, information, and skills you will need to achieve your goal. Especially identify the skills that you will have to develop to be in the top 10 percent of your field. Remember, to achieve a goal you've never achieved before, you're going to have to develop a skill and do something you've never done before. Your weakest key skill sets the limit on your income and your success. You can make more progress by going to work on the one skill that is holding you back than you can by working on any other.

   Here's the key question: what one skill, if you developed it in an excellent fashion, would have the greatest positive impact on your life? What one skill, if you were really good at it, would most help you to double your income?

   Once you answer this question, write it down, make a plan, and work on developing that skill every single day. Write down every book you could read, every audio program you could listen to, every action you could take, and every day do something that improves you in that one area.

6. Identify the people whose help and cooperation you will require to achieve your goal. Make a list of every person in your life that you will have to work with or work around to achieve a goal.

   Start with the members of your family whose cooperation and support you will require. List your boss, your coworkers, and your subordinates; especially identify the customers you will need to buy enough of your product or service to make the money you want.

Once you've identified the key people whose help you will require, ask yourself, what's in it for them? Be a go-giver rather than a go-getter. To achieve big goals, you will need the help and support of lots of people. One key person at a certain time and place in your life can make all the difference.

The most successful people are those who build and maintain the largest networks of other people whom they can help and who can help them in return.

7. Make a list of everything you will have to do to achieve your goal. Write down the obstacles that you will have to overcome, the knowledge and skills you will have to develop, and the people whose cooperation you will require. List every single step you can think of that you will have to follow to ultimately achieve your goal. As you think of new items, add them to your list until your list is complete.

   When you make a list of all the things you will need to do to achieve your goal, you will begin to see that it is far more attainable than you thought. Remember what Confucius said: "A journey of a thousand miles begins with a single step." You can build the biggest wall in the world, one brick at a time.

8. Organize your list into a plan. You accomplish this by arranging the steps that you have identified in two ways: first, by sequence, and second, by priority.

To organize a plan by sequence, ask what you have to do before you do something else, and in what order. To organize by priority, you ask what is more important and what is less important. The 80–20 rule says that 80 percent of your results will come from 20 percent of your activities. On the other hand, the 20–80 rule says that the first 20 percent of time that you spend planning your goal and organizing your plan will be worth 80 percent of the time and effort required to achieve the goal. Planning is very important.

9. Organize your list into a series of steps, from the beginning all the way through to completion. When you have a goal and a plan, you increase the likelihood of achieving your goals by 1,000 percent. Many statistics prove this. You cannot imagine the power of a written plan.

   Then plan each day, each week and each month in advance. Plan each month at the beginning of the month. Plan each week the weekend before. Plan each day the evening before. The more careful and detailed you are in planning your activities, the more you will accomplish in less time. The rule is that each minute spent in planning saves ten minutes in execution. This means that you get 1,000 percent return on your investment of time in planning your days, weeks, and months in advance.

10. Visualize your goals. Create clear, vivid, exciting, emotional pictures of your goals as if they were already a reality. See your goal as though it were already achieved.

Imagine yourself enjoying the accomplishment of this goal. If it's a car, imagine yourself driving this car. If it's a vacation, see yourself on the vacation already. If it's a beautiful home that you want, see yourself living in a beautiful home.

In visualizing, take a few moments as well to create the emotions that would accompany the successful achievement of your goal. A mental picture combined with an emotion has an enormous impact on your subconscious and your superconscious mind.

Visualization is perhaps the most powerful faculty available to you to help you achieve your goals faster than you ever thought possible. When you use a combination of clear goals, combined with visualization and emotionalization, you activate your superconscious mind. Your superconscious mind solves every problem on the way to your goal. It activates the law of attraction and begins attracting into your life the people, circumstances, ideas, and resources that will help you to achieve your goals faster.

A Goal Setting Exercise

Take a clean sheet of paper and write the word *Goals* at the top of the page, along with today's date. Discipline yourself to write out at least ten goals that you would like to accomplish in the next year or in the foreseeable future. Begin each goal with the word *I*. As I said, only you can use the word *I* with reference to yourself. Follow the word *I* with an action verb, which will act as a command from your conscious mind to your subconscious mind. For example, you could say, *I run, I earn, I sell, I achieve, I acquire, I save.* Following the word *I* with an action verb is like pushing down a dynamite detonator, which goes kaboom in your subconscious.

When you write your goals, describe them in the present tense, as if they all have been achieved. Your subconscious mind is only activated by the language of the present tense. If your goal is to earn a certain amount of money in a certain amount of time, you would say, *I earn this amount by this date.* If your goal is to get a new car, you would say, *I drive such and such a car by such and such a date.* This is a clear command from your conscious mind to your subconscious mind.

Again, when you write down your goals, always write them in a positive form. Instead of saying, *I will quit smoking,* you would say, *I am a nonsmoker.* Instead of saying, *I will lose weight,* you say, *I weigh this number of pounds.* Always take your goals as they were already a reality, as though you have already accomplished them. This activates your subconscious and superconscious mind to change your external so that it is consistent with your inner command.

Next, decide upon your definite major purpose. Once you have written a list of ten goals, ask yourself, if I could wave a magic wand and achieve any goal in this list within twenty-four hours, which one would have the greatest positive impact on my life? When your answer to that question, put a circle around that goal. Then transfer the goal to the top of a clean sheet of paper. Write it down clearly and in detail. Set a deadline on these goals, and set subdeadlines if necessary.

Identify the obstacles you have to overcome to achieve your goal. Identify the most important one, internal or external. Identify the knowledge and skills you will need to achieve your goal and the most important one that you'll have to excel at. Identify the people whose help and cooperation you require and think about what you can do to deserve their help. Make a list of everything you'll do to achieve your goal, and add to the list as you think of new things to do.

Organize your list by sequence and priority: by what you have to do first and by what is most important. Make a plan by organizing your list into steps from the first to the last. Then resolve to act on your plan every single day.

Plan your goals in terms of the activities you'll have to engage in to achieve it—daily, weekly, and monthly—in advance. Then discipline yourself to concentrate single-mindedly on the most important thing that you can do today until it is 100 percent complete. Do this with every major task. Resolve in advance that no matter what happens, you will never give up. Each time you persist and overcome the inevitable failures and disappointments, you become stronger and more resilient. You increase your self-esteem and self-conflicts. Your goal is to become unstoppable.

Decide exactly what you want, write it down, make a plan, and work on it every single day. If you do this over and over again until it becomes a habit, you'll accomplish more in the next few weeks and months than many people accomplish in several years or a life time. Begin today.

6

Time Management

One of the most important subjects for achieving goals, or for any kind of success in life, is time management. Here is the basic rule: time management is life management; it's really management of yourself. As business guru Peter Drucker said, "You can't manage time; you can only manage yourself." The most successful people are the ones who manage themselves the best.

The quality of your time management determines the quality of your life. I used to think that time management was a peripheral subject. I thought I was the sun, and time management was one of the planets that orbited around my life. The turning point came when I realized that time management is the sun, and everything else in life is a planet that goes around it. If you have your time completely under control, every other part of your life falls into alignment.

Time Management Is a Choice

The good news is that time management is a skill that can be learned and must be learned. Some say, "I'm not very good at time management. I'm not very punctual. I have too much to do and too little time." This is a choice you make.

Sometimes I joke with my audience. I say, "I've developed a method to teach people time management in just twenty seconds; I can make everybody here a brilliant time manager in just twenty seconds. Do you want to see my method?" They say, "Yes, yes." I reach into my pocket, as if I'm pulling out a pistol, and put it next to the head of a person in the front row. I say, "All right. I'm going to follow you around for the next twenty-four hours. If you waste a single second, I'm going to blow your brains out."

Under those circumstances, would you be a good time manager? You bet you would. The point is that time management is a choice. You *choose* to manage your time well. If you have to catch a plane, and that plane is really important, you will organize every part of your life so you are there in advance, ready to catch the plane.

You choose to be a good time manager. Once you understand that, you realize it's not genetic; it's not the way you were brought up; it's not the way you were as a kid. It's simply a decision that you make.

Your present situation in life is simple. First of all, you have too much to do and too little time. No matter how much you get done, you have even more to get done. Your workload and responsibilities continue to increase. This is a normal and natural fact of being an adult.

Here is the insight: you will never get caught up. Everybody has the idea that somehow they're going to find a technique or a method that will enable them to catch up. No, you'll never catch up. The only way to manage your time is to stop doing certain things.

Goals are the starting point of time management. They are the big picture: you stand back and you say, what are my real goals in life? What do I really want to accomplish? Because an enormous amount of our time is spent doing things that are irrelevant to our real goals.

Double Your Productivity

How do you double your productivity? Here are five steps:

1. Make a list of everything you have to do each day. Write this list out the night before, and never work without a list.

   According to time management specialists, a list will increase your productivity by 25 percent the first time you use it. If your productivity, performance, and output increase by 25 percent per year, you will double them every two years and eight months. If you double your productivity and output, you will double your results. If you double your results, you'll double your income. Simply by working from a list, increasing your productivity by 25 percent from the first day, you can double your income every two years and eight months, and then double it again and again.

2. Apply the 80–20 rule to your list before you begin. One of the most important words in time management is *consequences*. Something that has high consequences has high value. Something that has low consequences has low value.

3. Once you've made a list, and you've used the 80–20 rule and applied it to your list, use the ABCDE method. An A stands for something that you must do; it has serious consequences if you do it or don't do it. A B activity on your list is something that you should do; it has mild consequences. It might be making a phone call or checking in with somebody in the office. A C activity is nice to do but has no consequences at all: drinking a cup of coffee, reading the paper, surfing the Internet.

    Here's the rule: never do a B or C task when you have an A task left undone.

    The fourth letter in the ABCDE method is D, which stands for *delegate*. Delegate everything you can to anyone else who can possibly do it in order to free up more time for your A tasks.

    The final letter, E, stands for *eliminate*. Eliminate all activities that have low or no value. You do many things during the course of the day that, if you never did them at all, would make no difference.

    The more tasks you delegate and eliminate, the more time you have to do the things that make a difference in your life.

4. Ask four questions continually. The first is, why am I on the payroll? What have you been hired to do? If you were to go to your boss and ask this question, what specifically would your boss say. I can guarantee you that they would not tell you that you're on the payroll to get along well with your coworkers, surf the Internet, read the paper, or drink coffee. You're on the payroll to get specific results for which the company can pay you. These contribute to the results that your company has to achieve in order to survive and thrive in a competitive marketplace.

The second question you ask is, what are my highest-value activities? Of all the things you do, which ones are more valuable than anything else?

The third question is, what can I and only I do, which, done well, will make a real difference? In your work, there are certain things that only you can do. If you don't, nobody else will do them, and they won't get done. But if you do them and do them promptly and well, they can make a major difference in your life.

The answer to this question, by the way, changes with changing priorities and activities. Nonetheless, keep asking every minute, what can I and only I do, which, done well, will make a real difference?

Finally, keep asking, what is the most valuable use of my time right now? All time management books come down to answering that one question: what is the most valuable use of my time right now? Whatever it is, make sure that that's what you're doing every minute of every day.

5. The fifth key to doubling your productivity is to concentrate single-mindedly on one thing, the most important thing, and stay at it until it's 100 percent complete. Single-minded focus on your most important tasks saves as much as 80 percent of the time required.

    Concentrated, focused work on a single task is a source of energy, enthusiasm, and increased self-esteem. Closure and completion, getting a task finished, raises your self-esteem and motivates you to do even more.

    I write and produce four books a year. Professional writers are fortunate if they write or produce one book in two to three years. People ask, how can you write so many books? I focus and concentrate. When I sit down to write a book, I go through a series of steps. I concentrate single-mindedly on 100 percent completion of each step before I go on to the next. That's true for everything else I do, and it's astonishing how much you increase your productivity when you concentrate single-mindedly.

Creative Procrastination

Do you procrastinate? The answer is yes: everybody procrastinates. Unproductive people procrastinate, but so do highly productive people. The difference is that top people use creative procrastination: they procrastinate on things of low value, with no consequences. Unproductive people procrastinate on things of high value that can make a big difference in their lives.

Here are ten ways to overcome procrastination:

1. Set clear written goals and make written plans of action. The very act of writing things down often motivates you to get started. Once you do, like a rock rolling down a hill, you get going and you keep going.

2. Break your goals down into bite-sized activities. You know the old question: how do you eat an elephant? One bite at a time. If you can take a big goal and break it down into many tiny tasks, you can start by doing just one little task.

3. Look at what you have to do in the course of the day. Select one single activity and start on it immediately. Just motivate yourself to say, *I do this now. I do this now.* Starting immediately on one task will often break the mental logjam.

4. Swiss-cheese your tasks. Imagine a Swiss cheese with holes. Punch a hole in a task by selecting a small part of a big job and doing only that. Sometimes just taking one small piece of the task is enough to get you started.

5. Salami-slice a major job. Break a major job into a series of small slices, and do one piece of the job to get started.

6. Another way to overcome procrastination is to 20–80 the task. Sometimes the first 20 percent of time that you spend planning, organizing, and laying things out

is worth 80 percent of the whole job. You get everything organized, in place, planned, all your lists made. Sometimes that propels you into completing the job.

7. Set a time limit. Work on a major task for fifteen minutes. Say, "I can't do this whole job, because it takes many hours. I will work on this for fifteen minutes; then I'll do something else and come back to it later." Sometimes just working on a task for fifteen minutes gets you into the rhythm, and you don't want to stop.

8. Set up a reward structure. Give yourself a reward for completing part of a job. One activity in sales is prospecting: you have to pick up the phone and call people to arrange for appointments. Some salespeople will set a plate of cookies, broken up into small pieces, right in front of them. They'll say, "I will give myself a bite of cookie each time I contact the prospect. I'll give myself a coffee break after I've made ten appointments." Instead of worrying about the appointments, they train themselves to focus on the rewards, and they overcome their fear and their tendency to procrastinate in prospecting.

9. Make a promise to someone else. Tell them you will complete a task by a certain time. It's amazing how motivated you are to get something done when you want to keep your word.

10. Look at your list, and imagine that you are going to be called out of town for a month. You can only do one

thing on this list before you leave. Which will it be? Whatever it is, motivate yourself, drive yourself, into completing that one most important task. Usually this will propel you into completing every other task on your list as a result.

Getting More Done in a Day

Here are seven steps to getting more done during the day:

1. Work faster: pick up the pace, work at a higher tempo; a fast tempo is essential to success. Pick up your speed of walking, pick up your speed of working; move quickly; get on with it instead of dragging things out.

2. Work harder. Work longer hours. Start a little earlier, work a little harder, and stay a little later. Successful people work longer hours, they work productively during those longer hours, and they get vastly more done than the average person.

   I was recently reading about a woman who used to get up at five o'clock in the morning, exercise, start work at six, work for three solid hours, and have all her day's work done. She would work full-time without wasting any time. She would get all of the next day's work done as well.

   In time, this woman was doing the equivalent of three days of work every single day, simply by working longer hours. She kept being promoted and paid more until she was a senior executive and one of the highest-paid people in her company, simply because she worked longer, harder hours.

3. Work together; work with others on big tasks. Sometimes if you develop a production line rhythm or a delegation structure, you can do a certain task while someone else does another. You might be amazed at how much more you can get done.

4. Simplify the work. Eliminate steps so that you get more done faster. Consolidate or condense the work, get on with it, and get it done quickly. The simpler the work and the fewer the steps, the more you get done, and faster.

5. Do things that you're better at. When you do things that you're better at, you make fewer mistakes, which means you get more things done in a shorter period of time.

    For example, when I started off my career, I became a copywriter for a major advertising agency. I read book after book on writing copy and spent hours and hours writing advertising and promotional copy.

    Today in my company, when somebody needs a piece of copy for a brochure, a product, or a program, they send it on to me. I can whip out a piece of good copy in a few minutes. Someone else who is not a copywriter might work at it for hours, and it still wouldn't read right. I've ended up writing thousands of words of copy, much of which is, I'm happy to say, very good, because I'm very good at it. What are you very good at? What can you do in a short time, with few mistakes?

6. Bunch your tasks. Do a number of similar tasks at the same time. Use the learning curve. If you're going to write a series of proposals, do several at once. By the time you get to the fifth or sixth proposal, you are down to 20 percent of the amount of time it took you to do the first. If you're prospecting, by the time you do the tenth call, it's taking you about 20 percent of the time it took you to do the first call. When you bunch your tasks and do similar tasks together, you get faster and better at each one of them. You also save an enormous amount of time, with an equal or higher level of quality.

7. Get better at your key tasks. Practice the CANEI formula, which stands for *continuous and never-ending improvement*. One of the best time management skills ever developed is to get better at the most important things you do. The better you get, the more you can get done. Becoming excellent at what you do doesn't save you a few minutes or a few hours: it can save you years of hard work in getting to the same level of income.

All of these and other business skills are learnable. You can learn any skill you need in order to achieve any goal you can set for yourself. You can learn to be a superb time manager. One year from now, you can be so efficient and effective that television crews will be following you around because you're so good at what you do.

You could be only one time management skill away from doubling your income. You probably know what it is. Time management is really life management; it's management of yourself. It is the ability to choose the sequence of events—to choose what you do first, what you do second, and what you do not at all. And you are always free to choose.

7

Wealth Creation

Now that we've explored the best ways to work productively, we can turn to our ultimate long-term objective: wealth creation.

This is the best time in all of financial history to be
alive. With 5 percent of the world's population and 5 percent of the world's landmass, the United States produces
30 percent of the world's gross national product and owns
50 percent of the world's wealth. The United States has created more millionaires, multimillionaires, billionaires, and
multibillionaires in the last few decades than all the rest of
the world put together throughout history.

In 1900, there were five thousand millionaires in the
United States, most of them self-made. By the year 2000,
there were five million—an increase of a thousand times.
By 2008, the number of millionaires in the U.S. increased
to 9.6 million—an increase of 92 percent in eight years, the

largest expansion of personal wealth in history of man on earth. If anything, even more millionaires are going to be created in the years ahead. In 2020, the United States had a gross domestic product of around $20.93 trillion. In the first quarter of 2021, it grew at an annual rate of 6.4 percent—that's approximately $1.34 trillion per year. The average family income in the U.S. in 2019 was nearly $69,000, among the highest in the world, and continues to grow at 3–5 percent per annum, according to the Organization for Economic Cooperation and Development (OECD). The United States is the most entrepreneurial country in the world: more than two million new businesses are formed each year in the United States.

More people are making more money in more different ways than ever before. More people will become financially independent, if not self-made millionaires, in the next few years than in the last two hundred years put together. Your goal should be to become one of them. In this chapter, you will learn some of the most important principles of wealth creation.

What Millionaires Think About

You must be very careful about what you think about, especially with regard to yourself. What do self-made millionaires think about? Thousands of them have been interviewed. Most of them seem to have certain qualities in common: They think over the long term. They make efforts and sacrifices in the present in order to achieve financial independence ten and twenty years into the future. Unlike most people, they don't spend all their money and a little bit more besides. They practice the three keys to financial success—frugality, frugality, frugality—in their financial lives during their prime earning years so that they can achieve financial independence as early as possible.

Many people with average jobs, coming from average families, who practice frugality find themselves financially independent in their mid-forties or early fifties. Many people who make fabulous livings end up broke at the age of sixty or sixty-five. In Texas, they say, "Big hat, no cattle"— that is, he makes a lot of money, but he's got no assets.

Self-made millionaires develop the habit of enjoying the process of saving and accumulating rather than spending everything they make as they go along. They actually get pleasure from saving; they get pleasure from seeing their investments grow, as opposed to most people, who get their pleasure from going out and throwing their money around.

The Law of Three

The key measure of how well you are doing is your survival rate: the number of months or years that you could support your current lifestyle if you never worked again. Your goal should be to get your survival rate up to twenty years, and this amount becomes your number, your ultimate financial goal. To determine your number, calculate how much you need to live on each month, and then multiply that amount by 240: 20 years times 12 months. This becomes your long-term financial goal throughout your lifetime. This is your target.

The secret of wealth creation has been the same throughout history: add value. Everyone works on commission; everyone is rewarded by receiving a percentage of the value that they create with their work. The greater results that you get, the more value that you add, the greater your commission will be.

Most people start with nothing at the beginning of their careers. Virtually all wealth in America is first-generation. Moreover, almost all wealth begins with the sale of personal services; with sweat equity. To achieve financial success, you must continually seek ways to add value to whatever you are doing. Resolve to always put in more than you take out, to add more value than you charge. Always do more than you're paid for. Always go the extra mile in your work. As Napoleon Hill once said, "No one can ever stop you from putting in more than you're being paid for, from going the extra mile in everything you do, and it will put you on the side of the angels." There are never any traffic jams on the extra mile.

How do you add value in your work? You use the law of three. First, make a list of everything you do over the course of a week or a month at your job. You may end up with ten, twenty, or thirty large and small things that you do.

Second of all, review this list and ask yourself, if I could only do one thing all day long on this list, which one would contribute the greatest value to my business or my career? When I talk to salespeople, I have them ask which one activity would help them the most to double their income.

Third, once you've identified the one activity that contributes the most value, ask the question again: if I could only do two things all day long, what would be the second item?

Fourth, once you've determined your top two tasks, ask the question once more: if I could only do three things all day long, what would be the third?

In almost every case, your three key activities contribute 90 percent or more of all the value that you bring to your work. This is the law of three. The key to your success is to spend more and more time on those top three tasks and dedicate yourself to getting better and better at each of them.

Start Your Business Today

Eighty percent of self-made millionaires own their own businesses. They started with little or nothing, they built themselves up and achieved financial success as business owners. Another interesting statistic: fully 90 percent of businesses started by people with business experience eventually succeed, because they know what they're doing. On the other hand, fully 90 percent of businesses started by people with no business experience ultimately fail, at least in the short term.

Resolve to start your own business today, even if it's only a sole proprietorship. If you build it, they will come. When you start your own business, you will create a force field of energy that will attract into your life opportunities to activate this business.

Sometimes I tell people in my audiences to take out their business card, strike out the title, and write in the word *president*. Then strike out the company's name on the card and write in your own: John Smith Enterprises. You are now the president of your own company.

America is one of the easiest countries in the world to start a business. It takes an average of twenty-six hours and, using the Internet, between $25 and $50 for you to be in business. Start a business so you own a business even before you know what you're going to do with it.

You can form a sole proprietorship simply by naming it after yourself. If you name it after yourself, you don't even have to register the name to protect it. You do not need permission from anyone to start a sole proprietorship in your own name. If you want to start an S corporation, you can usually do this on the Internet at low cost. The advantage of a sole proprietorship or an S corporation is that everything you invest to start your business initially can be deducted against your income as a legitimate business deduction in the current year.

The IRS allows business owners to deduct expenses from their income, reducing the amount of tax they have to pay. As an employee with a paycheck, you don't get any of these deductions. As a business owner, you can deduct expenses that you would otherwise pay for with after-tax dollars, such as travel, gasoline, rent, automobile, and meals. For example, in 2021 the IRS allows you to deduct 56 cents per mile that you spend traveling with the hope of meeting people and doing business. If you drive 10,000 miles for business purposes, you can deduct $5,600 from your taxable income.

See yourself as the president of your own personal services corporation from now on. Starting your own business is actually a very simple thing. The key is this: simply find, create, acquire, or offer a product or service at a price that allows you to make a profit.

Please understand that in order to start a business, you have to sell something. People who start businesses are astonished at how much of their time they have to spend talking people into buying their product or service. Many of them hold back because they're afraid of selling. What if you're afraid of selling? You're only afraid because you don't know how, just as you may be afraid of skydiving or juggling with knives. Don't allow this lack of a learnable skill to hold you back from fulfilling all your financial dreams. Simply get a course, read a book, take a seminar, and learn how to sell effectively.

Say, *In order for me to start a business, I have to find something I can sell at a higher price than I paid for it.* That's been the starting point of every great fortune in history. All business, sales, and moneymaking skills are learnable. No one starts off with any of these important skills—doing a business plan, doing market analysis, writing advertising, budgeting, determining costs and prices, and promoting your business. Yet they're all learnable. Nobody starts off knowing them: they learn them over time. The faster you learn them, the sooner you will be successful.

Once you learn a business or sales skill, you can use it over and over again. Richard Branson, the serial entrepreneur from Britain, was once asked about this point. He said, "It's all pretty much the same. Once you understand the principles of starting and building a business, you can repeat it indefinitely in every other business." Branson has gone into music, airlines, hot-air balloons, and resort development. He takes the same principles, almost like a cookie-cutter recipe, and repeats them, and so can you.

Moreover, each time you use a business or moneymaking skill, you get better at it: you make fewer mistakes and get better results. As I mentioned, people who start businesses succeed at a rate of 90 percent if they have previous business experience. That's because they know what they're doing. People who start a business with no business experience don't know what they're doing and go broke. Your job is to gobble up business information, learn everything you can, not only before you start your business, but throughout your business career.

Courage and Skill

The key qualities required to start and build your own business, the major sources of wealth in our world today, are courage and skill. Everybody starts off with a lack of courage and a lack of skill. But when you do the thing you fear, the courage comes afterward. When you use the skill in which you are weak, the ability comes afterward.

It's important to understand this point, because many people think, "I'll make the call as soon as I have the confidence. As soon as I feel up and strong and courageous, I'll do it." No, that's not how it works. You do what you're afraid of, and the courage comes as a result. People say, "As soon as I feel good about prospecting or making calls or calling our customers, I'll get out there." No: you do it with the skill that you have, and additional skill comes afterwards. This is the key to success.

A vital part of success in business is to think through what you sell and whom you sell it to. Start off with the question that the owl asks in the dark woods: who? Who is your customer? Why would your customer buy your product? What does he consider to be a value? It's very important to understand who your customer is, and why they buy. What specific benefits does your customer seek in buying your product or service? Is it clear in your advertising, promotion, and presentation that your customer will receive these benefits?

Lack of clarity is the primary reason for sales failure. Fuzzy understanding is the greatest obstacle to closing. The prospect is unclear about how they will benefit by buying your product or service, so they say, "Let me think about it," which is another way of saying goodbye forever.

How does your product or service improve your customer's life or work? Remember that according to psychological studies, customers buy because of how they feel they will be afterwards. In other words, if I buy your product or service, what's the likely result? They project forward into the future, after the purchase. They must be able to see a clear state of improvement in their minds: they will be substantially better off by buying your product or service than with any other use of the money.

Here's a good question: why don't your customers buy from you? What holds them back? Why do they say no, if your product or service is obviously good for them? What in the customer's perception is causing them to hesitate? If you can identify that problem and remove it, you can often double your sales, double your income, build a successful business, and become financially independent.

Who are your competitors? Why does your customer buy from your competitor rather than you? What is the customer's perception? What does the customer see in your competitor that makes his choice more attractive than yours? How can you offset that? How can you minimize that? How can you replace it with something that you do better than your competitors?

What is your unique selling proposition? This is a benefit or advantage that you alone can offer to a customer and that he or she is willing to pay money for. What is your competitive advantage? What makes your product or service superior to your competitor's? What is your area of excellence? What does your product or service offer that is better than anything else that's out there?

These are the keys to business success. If you don't know what makes your product or service unique, if you don't know what makes you superior to your competitors—where you are excellent—you cannot even put together a basic sales presentation. You cannot write an ad. You cannot even identify the customer.

Once you start a business, dedicate 80 percent of your time and effort to selling; to new customer acquisition. Businesses succeed because of one thing: high sales. Businesses fail because of one thing: low sales. If you don't have a lot of money, start small, and test each step carefully.

Focus on Cash Flow

Grow slowly out of your cash flow and your profits. You don't have to sell your house and car and risk everything to start a business; you can start a small business with a small amount, and learn the necessary skills as you begin to grow.

Keep accurate records of all your transactions. Know where your money comes from and where it goes. Many companies will start a business: they'll buy a product or service for 50 cents and sell it for $1. They think they're making 100 percent profit, but at the end of the month, they're surprised to find they're losing money. They haven't taken into consideration gasoline, rent, utilities, staffing cost, postage, telephone cost, their own salary, meals. They don't realize that you can go broke on a 100 percent markup.

You need to know where your money comes from and where it goes. Again, make a list: write down every single penny that you spend and every single penny that comes in: that becomes the basis of your bookkeeping. Or, easiest of all, get yourself a bookkeeping system online, and punch in every single number every single day in the proper places.

Always concentrate your business on net profits, not gross sales volume. In other words, it's not the top line that matters, it's the bottom line. Focus on how much profit you will have at the end of the day. Make sure that what you're doing justifies the amount of work and investment that you put into it.

Always focus on positive cash flow. The most important number in any business is cash flow (sometimes called free cash flow). It is the lifeblood, the oxygen, to the brain of your business. If your cash flow is cut off for any period of time, your business can collapse overnight. Always be hypersensitive to cash flow.

The first rule for success in business is, don't lose money. One multibillionaire said his two rules for success are, number one, don't lose money. Number two is, if you're ever tempted, go back to rule number one. It's better to keep the money in the bank earning interest than to lose it, because when you lose money, you also lose all the time it took you to accumulate it in the first place. It's not just money you're losing, it's time—it's weeks and months and even years out of your life.

The Stock Market

Now let's talk about stock market investing, because that's very popular. Here are some of the rules based on exhaustive research.

Number one is, self-made millionaires do not make their money in the stock market. In fact, very few people make money in the stock market. Furthermore, 80 percent of stock market experts, with many years of experience, are unable to beat the stock market averages over time. Of the thousands of mutual funds, which are managed by the most astute financial managers in the world, 80 percent of them don't beat the averages. In other words, if you took a page of *The Wall Street Journal* with all of the New York Stock Exchange stocks, you threw darts at it, and you bought the stocks where the darts hit, you would do as well as 80 percent of the greatest financial minds working in the financial markets today.

Self-made millionaires do temporarily store their money in the stock market, usually in safe stocks with stable value. These are big, solid stocks, like Microsoft and Coca-Cola, that don't bounce up and down much because they sell products and services to large numbers of people.

Self-made millionaires spend an average of six minutes per day checking on their investments. If you ask the self-made millionaire, "How is your portfolio doing?" he has no idea, because he seldom even looks at it. He's just invested carefully and gets back to his main job.

Warren Buffett became one of the world's richest men by buying and trading stocks: he is the preeminent stock picker in history. With an estimated net worth of $108 billion in 2021, he recently wrote that there is nothing worth buying in the stock market today. That's because trading stocks does not add value. Going in and out of the market, buying and selling, doesn't add any value. The only way that you can acquire and achieve great wealth is by adding value in some way.

If you're going to invest in the stock market, the best of all investments is an index fund. These funds track the stock market, they outperform almost all mutual funds, and they have the lowest cost of acquisition and sales. They buy a little bit of all the stocks in a particular index. For instance, they'll buy a little bit of all the stocks in the Dow Jones or the Standard & Poor's or on a particular exchange, and your investment will simply track the averages.

Real Estate

Another key to money is real estate investing. The owner-
ship of income-producing real estate is a major source of
wealth in America. It is possible to buy real estate with no
money down, but you require a motivated buyer: someone who is anxious to sell and has no clear idea of what his
property is worth. A motivated buyer might be someone
who has to sell the house because he has just gone bankrupt, gotten a divorce, been transferred to another state, or
suffered a major loss. In other words, he's eager to get out of
the house and may not know what it's worth.

As for investing in real estate with no money down, real
estate experts will tell you that you must look at a hundred
properties before you can find ten on which you can make
an offer. Of these ten, you may be able to purchase one
property. It therefore requires several weeks or months of
hard work to find a property that you can buy for no money
down.

You must be careful even in buying foreclosures.
Remember, there is no such thing as easy money: you must
be very careful with every penny and be very concerned
about not losing money. Even if you can buy a foreclosure
with no money down, you still have to pay bank fees, mortgage fees, points at closing, closing fees, legal fees, title fees,
and a variety of other hidden expenses. All these have to be
paid in cash. Once you own the house, you have to pay all
the upfront cash costs of upgrading, renovating, landscap-
ing, repairs, and advertising in order to find a tenant. If you
don't find a tenant immediately, you must pay the monthly

operating and mortgage costs out of your own pocket until you do. Many homes or even office buildings that you'll buy at no money down will stay empty for six months, and you have to pay all of the expenses out of your pocket with cash.

One of the best methods to start in real estate is called *buy 'em, fix 'em*. This consists of buying a rundown house at below market price and fixing it up. Then you either rent it out or sell it and make a profit.

The first time you buy and fix up a house, it will take several months, even a year. The second time, it will take less time, maybe six months. After three years of experience, you can be buying, fixing up, and reselling four to six homes per year, making a profit each time, at little or no risk. I have met people who started off keeping their day jobs and went from house to house.

One couple told me the first house took a year; the second house took six months; the third house, two or three months; the fourth, two months; the fifth, one month. By the end of a year, they were buying, fixing up, renting out, or reselling a house every month and making about $20,000 to $30,000 per house, net.

This couple wasn't trying to make a million dollars. They worked on the weekends. Eventually they hired contractors who could do the work for them. They found bankers and financial institutions that would finance them. They had ads running continually to find tenants. They were building a substantial estate simply by buying and fixing up houses while they kept their day jobs.

You add value to real estate by making it more attractive so that you can rent it at a higher price, thereby increasing its market value. Or you can sell it and make a profit. The key to success in real estate is to think in the long term—the key quality of self-made millionaires. Never buy a piece of property with the idea that you're going to flip it and make a quick profit. Always think about owning a piece of property for five to ten years before you buy it in the first place.

Buying and flipping property is like playing musical chairs with real estate. When the music ends, somebody is left standing up without a chair. Today you find thousands and millions of people who were playing musical chairs and ended up with no chair. They ended up bankrupt, with their financial lives in ruin. Don't let this happen to you.

One key to success in real estate is to learn every detail about the property. When you buy a piece of property, imagine you're buying stock in that neighborhood, just as you would buy a stock in a company. Learn every detail about the property, the city, the neighborhood, the local economy, the local schools, shopping centers, and roads. Become intimately familiar with the property before you buy it. Really good real estate speculators will walk through the property and the neighborhood. They'll come at different times of the day, weekends, evenings, and so on. They'll listen for traffic noise; they'll look for traffic.

I bought my first house in the summertime. It was well priced. I thought I was getting a good deal. Then the leaves fell off the trees, and all of a sudden, the sound buffering disappeared. It turned out that there was a major freeway about a block and a half away. You could hear the roar of trucks, cars, and motorcycles twenty-four hours a day. You had to wear earplugs to sleep because of the noise.

Forever after, whenever I bought a property, I'd research the neighborhood carefully to make sure that there were no roadways that would drown the neighborhood in sound when the weather changed.

The Habit of Saving

Becoming financially independent is your long-term goal. The simplest way for you to accomplish this is to develop the habit of saving 10 to 20 percent of your income throughout your lifetime.

If you're starting off in debt today, as most people are, begin by saving 1 percent of your income and living on the other 99 percent. Once you become comfortable living on 99 percent, increase your savings rate to 2 percent of your income, then 3 percent, 5 percent, and eventually 10 percent. Within a year or so, you will be living quite comfortably on 80 to 90 percent of your income, saving and investing the balance. If you do this throughout your working lifetime, you will become a millionaire.

This method works, by the way, because human beings are creatures of habit. You get into a habit of spending the amount of money that you're earning. But if you pay yourself first, off the top, and save that money, you get into the habit of living on what you have left. Pretty soon, what seems to be a little difficult at the beginning becomes very comfortable. Then your financial estate begins to grow.

Self-made millionaires develop the habit of living within their means. The key to financial success can be summarized in five words: *spend less than you earn*. Spend less than you earn, and invest the difference.

Five Don'ts for Financial Success

There are five don'ts for financial success:

1. Don't seek easy money or get led astray by get-rich-quick-schemes and ideas.
2. Don't look for rewards without working. All people who achieve financial success work hard for a long time.
3. Don't expect someone else to do it for you: you are responsible.
4. Don't trust luck or hope for miracles. They never occur in financial matters.
5. Don't expect to be successful the first time. You will make hundreds of little mistakes on the way to developing the wisdom and experience that you need to get and keep a financial fortune.

Five Dos for Financial Success

Let me end this chapter with five dos for financial success:

1. Study and understand every aspect of any investments you make for the rest of your life. If you don't understand an investment, don't put your money into it.
2. Continually look for ways to add and increase value in every situation.

3. Be prepared to get rich slowly. All serious money is long-term, patient money.

4. Be frugal with your money at all times. Be careful and thoughtful about how you invest it and spend it; continually watch your money like a hawk.

5. Resolve today to get your savings rate up to 10 to 20 percent of your income for the rest of your life, and then invest that money carefully. Finally, don't lose money.

All moneymaking skills are learnable. You can learn anything you need to learn to achieve any goal you can set for yourself. Almost everyone who is wealthy today started off poor. By studying what other financially successful people have done in the past and doing the right things over and over, you will eventually get the same results. You will eventually achieve the financial independence you desire and hope for.

8

How to Become a Millionaire

I've already pointed out that there are more opportunities for people to become millionaires in the years ahead than ever before, but the basic rules for becoming a millionaire have never changed.

Spend Less than You Earn

As I emphasized in the previous chapter, spend less than you earn, and save or invest the balance. Some years ago, I was doing a seminar on financial success and achievement. At the break, several well-dressed people were standing around me at the bottom of the stage. A young man came pushing through the crowd. He was obviously not all together: he was dressed poorly, and as soon as he began to speak, it was clear that he had a mental problem. He said, "Mr. Tracy, can I be a success too?" I didn't know what to say to him. Then he went on to speak. He said, "Mr. Tracy, I live in a group home." Which tells you what his life situation was like. He said, "We repair furniture." Which told you his level of competence. "Mr. Tracy," he said, "every month, I save $100. If I do that, will I be a success?"

As it happened, the day before I'd been reading compound interest tables, which I don't read that often. I found that if you saved $100 a month, you invested in a good mutual fund that increased at 10 percent per annum, and you did that from age twenty to age sixty-five, you'd be worth $1,118,000. That young man, with no advantages going for him at all, had been given some good advice by someone. He saved $100 a month from his earnings, and he would end up one of the richest people in society. He'd end up richer than doctors, lawyers, architects, engineers, and businesspeople who did not save as much as he did. As Albert Einstein said, "Compound interest is the most powerful force in the universe."

Investing $100 a month on a regular basis will make you rich. Think what $200 or $300 or $500 a month would do. Spend less than you earn, pay yourself first, save 10 percent off the top of every paycheck, and live on the rest. If you can't do this, as I said in the previous chapter, start with 1 percent and live on 99 percent until you develop the habit and it becomes easy and automatic for you to live on less.

When I was a young man and was just starting off, Lloyd Conant, the founder of the Nightingale-Conant audio company, said, "Brian, you have the potential ability to earn a lot of money in life. Remember this: it's not how much you earn, but how much you keep that counts."

How do you keep your money? Simple: delay, defer, procrastinate on every expenditure. If you're thinking about buying a house, a car, or a boat or taking a trip, give yourself thirty days to decide. Never be rushed into a big expenditure, even if it's a stereo. The most amazing thing happens: if you think about a big expenditure for a while, your desire to buy it will drift away. You think, "You know, I might be better off saving that money, putting it into something that grows rather than spending it at this time."

This is the mindset of self-made millionaires. Never buy new when you can buy used. Studies of self-made millionaires show that they never buy new cars. Why? Because if you buy a new car, you lose 30 percent of the car's value when you drive it off the lot, because of depreciation. Self-made millionaires buy good cars that are two or three years old; all the depreciation is out of them, but they're still under warranty. They'll buy a car and drive it for ten years until it falls apart. They'll take all the money that people use to buy new cars, and they'll buy property, invest carefully in their business, and put the money where it grows. If you were to just buy a used car every ten years and drive it till the wheels fell off, take all that extra money, and invest it carefully, that would give you a quantum leap toward financial independence.

Track Your Spending

Count your pennies, and the dollars will take care of themselves. A recent study showed that people who track their expenditures save 50 percent more than people who don't.

Keep a little spiral notebook in your pocket. Every time you spend money on something, write it down. Psychologists have found that writing something down brings it to your awareness: you're much more attentive to it. If you buy a double frappé, nonfat cappuccino latte at a café for $4.35, you write it down. If you buy a newspaper or a Coke, you write it down; if you go out for lunch, you write it down. As you do this and you track your numbers, you automatically start to spend less. People who do this for one month find themselves spending 50 percent less, because many of the expenditures we make are mindless; we don't even think about them.

Add Value

As I've already said, all wealth comes from adding value in some way. You add value by doing more important things: you find the things that are most important to your customers and do those things for them. You add value by doing things faster, cheaper, better. This is the key to success in business: faster, cheaper, better. Every single day, look for a way to serve your customers faster, cheaper, better.

You also add value by reducing costs and by giving people more of what they want and need at prices they're willing and able to pay. Remember the famous quote from motivational speaker Zig Ziglar: "You can get everything you want in life if you just help other people get the things that they want." That's the key to becoming wealthy.

Where Millionaires Come From

Where do self-made millionaires come from in America? Entrepreneurs make up 74 percent of them. Look at your great entrepreneurs: Bill Gates; his partner, Paul Allen; Warren Buffett; Larry Ellison; Michael Dell; Sam Walton—they all started with nothing. They started their own businesses with a little bit of money and a lot of sweat equity. (Actually, the number one source of millionaire entrepreneurship is cell phone businesses.)

The second source of self-made millionaires, 10 percent, is well-paid executives: people who work for large companies and are well paid, get stock options, and hold on to their money.

The third category of self-made millionaires, another 10 percent, consists of professionals—doctors, lawyers, architects, engineers—who are successful in their practices and accumulate money.

The next group—5 percent of self-made millionaires—are salespeople. Maybe they worked for the same company or for many companies, but they sold all their lives. They made a lot of money, and they put the money away and held on to it.

What's the most important skill for attaining wealth? Sales.

Success in entrepreneurship is based on your ability to start a business and sell something. If you combine the categories of entrepreneurs and salespeople—74 percent plus 5 percent—you see that 79 percent of individuals have become millionaires through sales.

The last 1 percent of non-inherited wealth comes from all other sources: writers, movie stars, inventors. From the newspapers and magazines, you may think that these are the primary source of wealth in America. People who accidentally stumble into money or win a lottery or become rock stars are very rare. Almost all of your potential for success rests on your ability to start a business and sell a product or service.

Qualities of Millionaires

The number one quality of self-made millionaires is *honesty*. Earl Nightingale used to say that if honesty did not exist, it would have to be invented as the surest way to getting rich. The reason is simple: all business is based on trust. Nobody can succeed in business unless everybody trusts them. Their customers have to trust them when they sell their products or services; their staff has to trust them; the bank has to trust them; their suppliers have to trust them. You will find that businesspeople are some of the most honest people you'll ever meet. When a businessperson is dishonest, it gets into the newspapers. But out of twenty-six million businesses in America, only a tiny fraction are actually dishonest, because if you are dishonest in business, you're finished. You have to move to another country; you can never start again, because your integrity has been compromised.

The second quality of self-made millionaires is *self-discipline*. After decades of research, Napoleon Hill concluded that self-discipline is the master key to riches: the discipline to make yourself do what you should do when you should do it, whether you feel like it or not. Discipline is the key. Get yourself up in the morning, get yourself working, concentrate on high-priority tasks, pay the price of success, and advance. I'll say more about self-discipline in chapter 10.

The third quality of self-made millionaires is *getting along well with others*. To be successful, self-made millionaires have to please a large number of people. They're likable; people like them and are willing to buy from them; people are willing to work with them and for them; people are willing to lend them money. Taking the time to be nice to people is extremely important.

Furthermore, most self-made millionaires have *supportive spouses*. Having a spouse who stands behind you saves an enormous amount of energy. You're not spending half of your life going out on dates. All the energy that you would spend on a problem marriage or relationship or on finding a partner is available for you to focus on your business. Behind almost every self-made millionaire or billionaire, there is a woman who supports him all the time. Behind almost every self-made female millionaire or multimillionaire, there's a strong man as well.

The fifth quality of self-made millionaires is that they are *hard workers*. In interviews with tens of thousands of them, they were asked how they managed to accumulate a million dollars in one lifetime. Eighty-five percent of them said the same thing: "I wasn't the sharpest one in school. I didn't get good grades. I saw that a lot of people had more going for them than me, but I was willing to work harder than they were. They weren't willing to work as hard as I was."

At a recent conference, the president of a large national corporation told a motivational story about a friend of his who had won seven Iron Man triathlons in Hawaii in a row. This is the toughest triathlon in the world: you have to run 26.4 miles, swim 3.5 miles, and ride a bicycle 125 miles. The president asked his friend, "How could you run and win that many triathlons in the greatest competition in the world?" His friend replied, "Well, a lot of them have better physical structure than me, but I win because they're not willing to take the pain that I'm willing to take."

Isn't that the reason for success? Successful people are willing to take the pain—the long nights, the long weekends, the worry, the stress, the difficulty—and keep on kicking on.

The sixth quality of self-made millionaires is that *they do what they love to do*. Most self-made millionaires will tell you, "I never worked a day in my life. I just do what I love to do, and I get paid well for it."

As you experiment and try different jobs and careers, look for something you really enjoy. If you are in sales, look for a product that you love, that you use, that you are excited about. Look for customers you love to sell to, look for markets you love to work in, so that when you go to work, you're happy all the time.

You'll find it essential for your success to do something that you love. Offer a product you love, sell to people that you really care about. If that doesn't fit the description now, try something else. It doesn't mean that you're the wrong person; it may just mean that you're in the wrong place at this time.

Rich Dad, Poor Dad

My good friend Robert Kiyosaki is famous for his Rich Dad, Poor Dad philosophy. He puts people into four categories. The first category is *employees*. They work for a salary. They don't get any tax benefits, aside from what comes off their paycheck. It's very hard for a person working for a salary to achieve financial independence. As my friend Mark Victor Hansen says, "They have a job, and the word *job* stands for *just over broke*."

The second category of people is the *self-employed*. These are independent contractors; they work on commissions; they work on income; they work on bonuses, but they're lone wolves.

The third category is *entrepreneurs*. These are lone wolves as well, but they have people working for them who are doing specialized tasks, so they get more done than they would as individuals.

The fourth group of people is *investors*. They invest their money to create income sources, or what we call passive income. They invest in a company or a business that is run by others and throws off steady profits, such as oil wells or commercial or residential real estate.

Wealth is income from other sources. I have a good friend who came over from Lebanon many years ago, unable to speak English, and is now worth an enormous amount of money. One day years ago, he asked me, "Brian, how much money do you make?"

I said, "Well, I'm doing pretty well."

"I would guess, based on my knowledge of your business, that you're making about this amount of money." He was pretty accurate. He asked, "How many wealth sources do you have aside from your work?"

"What do you mean?"

"If you stopped working, how much money would you have?"

"If I stopped working, if it would all stop. It would be like a car coming to a halt when it runs out of gas."

"Then you're not wealthy at all. You're making lot of money, but you're not wealthy. You're only wealthy when you have money coming in whether you work or not."

That was like a slap in the face with a wet fish. I changed my entire financial life. I began thinking more seriously about developing assets, investing, and so on, because wealth is money in the mailbox. Wealth is money that comes in whether you work or not.

In the Rich Dad, Poor Dad philosophy, your goal is to move from employee (by saving your money) to self-employed (by working on commission) to entrepreneur (by having people work for you) to investor (where your money works for you, and the money comes in whether you work or not).

The rule in life is that you start off with nothing (as is the tradition in American society). It's like lining up for a big marathon. Everybody starts off running: some people will win, some people will stay back in the pack, some people will come in after everybody's gone home.

You start out with lots of time, but no money. Over the course of your working lifetime, your goal is to change that ratio, so that you have less time as you get older but more money. You finally cross over to the point where your money is earning more than you are; at that point you can resign and work full-time managing your money. That's your goal. Early in life, you trade time for money; later in life, you trade money for time.

Keys to Personal Financial Planning

Here are some keys for personal financial planning.

The first is *targeting*. Targeting means that you set clear financial goals for your life. You determine your annual income goal this year, next year, and the year after. You determine your monthly savings goal. How much are you going to save each month? Write it down on the upper right-hand corner of a piece of paper.

The very act of writing these numbers down makes it much more likely that you will actually achieve them. (If you have no idea about an annual income goal, see what you earn at the end of the year when you get your W-2 form.) If you have no idea of a monthly savings goal, you'll have a natural tendency to spend the money.

How much do you want to be worth each month and each year? Have clear targets: you can't hit a target that you can't see.

The second step is *taking stock*. Work out your net worth. How much are you worth today exactly? How much do you owe exactly? What is your current net worth? What would you be worth today if you had to sell everything? Go through your entire financial life, and make a list. Imagine that you had to sell all your assets and move to another country; you have to have a fire sale, a swap sale, or garage sale. How much would you have if you had to sell everything?

Some people may say, "I've got $100,000 worth of furniture." But if you had to sell your furniture, how much could you get for it? The answer is 10 cents on the dollar. If you had to sell most of your personal possessions, you'd be lucky to get 10 or 20 cents on the dollar. Be honest: how much you really worth today, and what is your goal for retirement?

Analyze your current situation. Write down how much you have today on the bottom left-hand corner of the page. Up at the right-hand corner, you have your goal for retirement. Draw a line between the two. That tells you how far you have to go to accumulate twenty times your annual costs.

The third key is *trimming*, reducing your expenses. Carefully calculate every expense and evaluate it before you spend the money. Before you make an expenditure, write it down, think about it, and talk about it with others. Don't spend impetuously. Procrastinate about buying large items. Examine your biggest monthly expenses, and look for ways to reduce or eliminate them.

People usually buy or rent the biggest home that they can afford. But as of June 2021, Warren Buffett was worth over $108 billion. He lives in the same house he started off in thirty years ago and drives the same car he drove ten years ago. Before he died, Sam Walton was driving a pickup truck he'd been driving for ten years. This attitude toward money spilled over into everything these men did: they constantly looked for ways to reduce expenditures. You need to do the same thing.

The fourth part is, *make yourself more valuable.* Concentrate on your hourly rate. What is your hourly rate today? You get your hourly rate by taking your annual salary or income and dividing it by 2,000 (the average number of hours worked in a year). For example, if today you are earning $50,000 a year, your annual income divided by 2,000 comes down to $25 an hour. Deciding to double your income means doubling your hourly rate to $50 an hour. What can you do to increase your value so that somebody will willingly pay you $50 an hour?

That takes us back to the law of three: what are the three things that you do that contribute the most value and how can you get better and better at those three things? Apply the 80–20 rule to your work. What are the 20 percent of things that you do that contribute the greatest value? How could you do more of those all day long?

Finally, be prepared to change jobs. A young man who said he was twenty-five came up to me at a seminar. He said, "You know, I want to improve my life, but I am a plumber. I've spent several years getting my journeyman ticket. I work for a plumbing company, but all the guys in this company who make money are the salespeople. They sell plumbing supplies to contractors."

"Why don't you become a salesman?" I said.

"Will I have to give up my training?"

"Look," I said. "Forget about your training. Your most important responsibility is to earn the most you possibly can. You know lots about plumbing. You have a lot in common with the people you're talking to."

"I never thought about that, but I don't know how to sell."

"You can learn to sell by listening to audio programs, reading books, and going to courses."

He said, "By God, I will."

About two years later, the man came up to me and said, "Remember me? I was a plumber. You told me to change jobs, so I did. I am making triple what I was earning as a full-time plumber. I've never made so much money in my life. I've got a better house for my kids, a better car, a better life; we take better vacations. Thank you very much for your advice."

Some jobs have a ceiling. Sometimes you've hit the ceiling. No matter how hard you work, or how good you are, the company won't pay you any more. It's time to find a better job. Now you're prepared for it. Now you're a good catch. Now you're the kind of person that employers will want to hire.

9

The Keys to Entrepreneurship

As we saw in the previous chapter, 74 percent of the self-made millionaires in America are entrepreneurs. Consequently, entrepreneurship—starting your own business—is your most likely route to financial success.

You need several things to start your own business. The first is *competence*. You must be very good at what you do. People will only buy from those who they feel can serve them better than anyone else. You must take it as a personal affront if somebody says that your competitor's products or services are better than yours. Concentrate on joining the top 10 percent. Concentrate on becoming excellent at what you do.

The second key to starting your own business is *customers*. Your first job is to get a customer. Your second job is to get a customer. Your third job is to get a customer. Your job is to get customers all day long and never take your eye off the customer ball. Customers are the key to business success. As I've said, successful companies have high sales, and unsuccessful companies have low sales; all else is commentary.

The third C is *cash flow*. This is the life of the business. Successful businesspeople think about their cash flow all the time. I know exactly, to the penny, how much comes in and out of my business every single day. I have a complete report on where all the money is every single day. I have a complete report of every sale and every dollar from every sale, every expense and every bill, every single day. I keep eyes on the cash flow as a doctor would keep their hands on the pulse of a critically ill patient. It's very important that you do that. As motivational speaker Jim Rohn said, "Casualness brings casualties."

How to Start

Before you get into a business, study and learn it in every detail. Work in the business, at least for a day or two. Work on the weekends, work in the evenings, and work for free. Just say, "You know, I'd like to learn about the business. Can I work for free?" People won't turn you down; they'll say, "Sure, come on in."

Once you're in, ask, "Why do you do this? Why do you do that? How does this work?" Many people have tried out a business this way. After a few hours or a few days, they'll say, "This is not the business for me." Or, "I like this business. I think I can do it well."

Subscribe to the publications in your business field, and read them. Go to the conferences and trade shows, and attend the talks given by the best people.

I have a friend who came over from England as an immigrant, and to get by, he sold advertising space for a small publication. It went broke. He went to work for another publication, which also went broke. He said, "I could publish a magazine." He looked around. People had asked him, "Why isn't there a magazine on sports and fishing in this state?" He thought, "I'll start a magazine on sports." He started a little magazine, and he began to sell advertising: that was his skill. He had people write up the stories while he sold the advertising.

About a year into this project, my friend was a little guy with his little publication, working out of his house, and just getting by. He went to a conference for magazine publishers in New York and attended a lecture on accounting for spa publications. The speaker said, "When you take your statement of accounts, and you have your sales at the top, then you have all your expenses, and you deduct those, what is this line called at the bottom of the page?"

Everybody said, "That's your bottom line."

"What does that represent?"

"That represents your profits or losses."

"Yes, this is how most people do it. I want you to do it differently. I want you to flip it over: make your bottom line your top line. Across the top, write the profits that you intend to make each month. Below that, write the sales that you will have to make to generate those profits, and then the costs that you'll incur. Start with your profits, rather than ending up with them—if you're lucky."

My friend walked out of that lecture and never looked back. Today he owns twenty-nine publications. He's a multimillionaire, one of the most respected people in the country. He's never lost money in a single month on any publication, which is unheard of in the magazine industry. It was all because of that one lecture that he attended at that one conference from that one accountant who had the one idea.

I tell you this story because you never know where that idea is going to come from. You have to expose yourself to a lot of good ideas. You've got to go where the ideas are. If you want to catch fish, fish where the fish are. If you want to learn how to run your business well, go to where other people in your field are talking about how to run a business well. Read, listen, learn, talk, and ask for advice.

Expand out of Your Profits

Start small and expand out of your profits. Somebody might say, "I can't get a bank loan to start a business." Of course you can't. Banks do not lend money to business startups. Neither do venture capitalists. Nobody gives money to startups. Ninety-nine percent of all new businesses are funded by love money. Love money is your own money, because you love your idea, and money from your friends and relatives, because they love you. Therefore, start small with a little money, sell something, make a profit, and then do it again.

A great way to start a business—millions of people have done this and become wealthy—is in network marketing. Network marketing offers wonderful products and services—health, beauty, home care products, and so on—that are usually of very high quality. Instead of selling them through retail outlets, which have to be supplied by wholesale outlets, which have to be supplied by jobbers, companies take the money that they would normally pay in commissions and markups and give it to the network marketing chain. They can pay as much as 40, 50, or 60 percent of the total retail price. They'll pay it back to the people who sell it one person at a time.

Network marketing is a now $140 billion business worldwide and growing like brushfire. You can start with a few $100. You can grow your business out of your own results, out of your own sweat equity. That's a great place to start.

The critical thing about network marketing is to sell something that you like, that you believe in, that you use yourself and benefit from, and that you feel that other people would enjoy and benefit from as well. If you can do that, you'll be a great salesperson for your product.

Learn the Ropes

You can also start in someone else's business and learn the ropes. Interested in getting a Burger King franchise? You have to work for four hundred hours in a Burger King. After you've applied for the franchise, you have to work at every single part of the business until you are immersed in hamburgerology (yes, they call it that) and say, "Yes, this is the business I want to be in." Enormous numbers of people who say, "I want a Burger King franchise" bail after they've worked in an outlet, because they realize it isn't right for them. The best time to find out that a business deal is wrong for you is before you get into it.

Once you get started, use brains and energy rather than capital and investment to get going. Whenever you possibly can, use creativity, intelligence, hard work, character, and personality, rather than investing money. A couple of years ago, on the way to a talk I was giving to a thousand potential entrepreneurs, I stopped by a bookstore and found a book called *1,001 Businesses You Can Start for Less than $100*. There was page after page after page. People say to me, "I don't have enough money to start a business," but there are over a thousand businesses you can start for less than $100 and grow out of your own efforts.

The key to success in every business is sales ability, and sales ability is learnable. You can have an average company with an average product, and you can have an average background, but if you're a great salesperson, you're going to be rich. You could have the best product and market and demand, but if you're not skilled in sales, you'll worry about money all your life.

Create a business plan before you start. A business plan asks you a whole series of questions about your product, customers, market, financing, advertising, promotion, production, service, standards, accounting, and everything else. It forces you to ask the critical questions that will make or break your business. (By the way, you can just go on the Internet, download a business plan template, and fill in the blanks.)

Many people put together a business plan and realize, "I thought that was a great business idea, but I can't get there from here. Now that I've answered these questions, it's not a good idea at all. There are not enough customers to pay the price I have to charge. There are not enough customers that I can get to switch from what they're currently using." A business plan helps you think these things through before it's too late.

Once you start, focus 80 percent of your time on sales and marketing. Forget about accounting. Forget about book-keeping. Forget about packing boxes. Forget about loading trucks. Spend 80 percent of your time hammering away at the market. This is more important than anything else.

Practice frugality in all things. Successful business-people are very cheap; unsuccessful businesspeople throw their money around. During the dot-com, dot-bomb explosion in Silicon Valley, people were getting enormous amounts of venture capital funding before they even had a company going. They blew the money on incredible things. One group of entrepreneurs put together a dot-com company. They decided to raise capital by having an extravaganza in Las Vegas, and they invited venture capitalists from all over the country. They spent $13 million on a one-night extravaganza, even though they only had $14 million to start with. They bankrupted the company, and the owner went to jail for embezzlement.

Be really tight with your money; get used furniture and equipment; use secondhand offices. Buy things very carefully, only when you need them, and only in the quantity that you require right now. Act as though your business is on the verge of bankruptcy all the time, and look for ways to keep your costs low and tight.

Finally, learn from every mistake and experience. You'll find that all business is trial and error. When you start a new business, you will make an enormous number of mistakes. That's to be expected. Stop after every experience and say, "What have we learned from this? What is this telling us that will help us to be better and smarter next time?"

When you talk about the lessons, everybody will be positive, everybody's dimmer switch will go on full, and people become more creative.

As I suggested earlier, use the two magic questions: *What did we do right in this situation? What would we do differently next time?*

Borrowing from the Bank

Everybody talks about borrowing from the bank. The first thing you have to know is that banks survive and thrive by making good loans to customers who will pay them back promptly.

Please understand this: when you talk to a banker, the banker does not see you as a person, but as a source of revenues for the bank. The bank lends you the money at a higher rate than they pay. The success or failure of the person across the counter is determined by whether or not they have made good loans. If they have made good loans, they get promoted. If they make bad loans, they get fired and blackballed from the banking industry.

When a banker is looking at you, they're very cautious. Bankers, as you can imagine, are not high-risk people. In fact, banks are not in the business of taking risks.

When they evaluate a loan, as a banker once told me, they look at five things, the five C's:

1. **Credit rating**. They can turn to their computer, put in your name, and get your credit rating from three scoring companies in two seconds, and they can print it out. Your credit rating tells them how much they can lend you or not, based on bank regulations, and how much they have to charge you for the loan. Sometimes it can be quite high. That's why your credit rating is personal. Be fastidious about your credit rating, because it's the starting point of every cent that you borrow for the rest of your life.

2. **Collateral: other assets**. I went to a bank once to borrow money for my company. They said, "What else have you got?"

   "What do you mean, what else?" I said. "My company."

   "No, we don't look at your company as an asset, because if your company is not successful, it will have no value. We want to know if you've got a house, a car, investments in property, and so on." They wanted a list of every single asset that I had before they would lend me any money.

The bank wants collateral well in excess of the amount that you are asking to borrow for your business. In fact, this banker told me that when someone comes to the bank for the first time, they want $5 of collateral for every dollar they lend, just in case things go wrong.

3. **Cash flow.** Bankers want to know all the money that you have coming into your company, and all other sources of cash flow that can be used to service the debt. They aren't just concerned about your company; they want to know how much your wife makes and how much you have coming in from an insurance policy or an investment or bond. They want every penny on the table.

4. **Commitment.** How much of your own money have you invested? How much do you have on the table?

   If you haven't put in all of your own money, they'll be reluctant to lend you any of theirs.

5. The last thing bankers look for is your **character**, your reputation. Do you have a good reputation? Are you known in the community as a person who pays their debts? Very often the size of your character will overwhelm all the others. If people know that no matter what happens, you always pay your debts, they will be much more willing to lend you money.

Good Chemistry

Visit several banks if necessary to find a banker who will work for you. It's just like when you decide to get married: make sure that you've got good chemistry. When you decide to work with a bank, make sure that you get along really well with the banker. You may have to go out on several "dates" before you find the right one.

Then keep your banker informed of any changes. If there's ever a time when you cannot pay your bills, let the banker know. Invest a lot of time and effort to build the relationship, and then make sure the relationship stays solid.

Here's the rule: bankers hate surprises. They hate to find out that you cannot make your monthly payments of interest or principal. They need to know about it well in advance.

I got into serious trouble some years ago, and I found that a bank loan is always current as long as the interest is paid. I had been committed to paying principal and interest every month, so I went to the banker and said, "Look, I've got a bit of a shortfall here, but I will maintain the interest payments."

He said, "That's OK; we understand that."

Banks understand that companies have problems. I have always kept my interest current, and I always kept my credit rating above 800. So if you run into trouble and you can't make principal and interest payments, offer at least to make interest.

Protecting Your Assets

The rule is, if you have money, you're going to get sued. There are thousands of lawyers who make their money by trolling. They look for anybody anywhere who has money that they can be sued for, for any reason. If you get sued, even with the most ridiculous lawsuit, you have to defend against it. You can't say, "I'm just going to ignore it." No. If you get sued, you have to get your own lawyer, and you have to fight it.

The best piece of advice I've learned from the experts in asset protection is to form a family limited partnership: a FLP. You use this to act as a firewall around your assets: you throw all of your assets over the wall so that they are protected inside. You transfer all your assets, your home, your car, your business, everything into the FLP, which is owned by you and the members of your family. Have your life insurance policy owned by a separate life insurance trust, so it's untouchable. Draw up a will that allocates your estate clearly, and update it annually. Don't leave anything to chance with regard to a will.

To protect your assets, insure sufficiently. Make sure that you have fire, theft, liability, flood, and health insurance. Have insurance for anything that you can't write a check to cover. Many people will actually lose everything because they insured improperly.

Finally, use a good lawyer to draw up proper contracts, trusts, wills, and business agreements. I got into a legal problem some years ago, which led to a lawsuit that dragged on for two or three years and cost hundreds of thousands of dollars. I went to a lawyer and showed him the contract I was being sued for. He said, "Brian, who drew up this contract?"

I said, "I did."

He said, "Brian, don't be so cheap next time. Spend a few hundred or a few thousand dollars to have a lawyer go over it, because they know where all the bodies are buried. They know the little sub clauses that can trip you up and make you vulnerable to a lawsuit. Brian, don't ever be cheap like this again."

I never was. Boy, does it make a difference. Pay a few dollars for a lawyer to protect you.

10

Self-Discipline

In the stages of the Phoenix Transformation so far, I've alluded to the importance of self-discipline, and in this chapter, I will develop this idea further.

Your ability to develop the habit of self-discipline will contribute more to your success than any other quality of character. Some years ago, I met a noted success authority named Kop Kopmeyer, who had discovered a thousand success principles, which he had published in four books containing 250 principles each. I asked him which principle he considered to be the most important. He said immediately that it was self-discipline, which he defined as the ability to make yourself do what you should do when you should do it, whether you feel like it or not.

Napoleon Hill, after interviewing five hundred of the richest people in America, also concluded that self-discipline is the master key to riches. Al Tomsik, the famous sales trainer, said, "Success is tons of discipline." Jim Rohn said, "Discipline weighs ounces, but regret weighs tons."

Dr. Edward Banfield of Harvard concluded that long-term perspective was the key to upward social and economic mobility. Over fifty years of research, he discovered that people who succeeded greatly were able to delay gratification in the short term so that they could enjoy greater rewards in the long term. When making decisions for current actions, they thought ten and twenty years into the future.

The Key Word: Sacrifice

The key word here is *sacrifice*. This is why saving and investing in the present is the first key to becoming financially successful in the future. Self-discipline means self-control, self-mastery, and the ability to have dinner before dessert. It doesn't mean that you don't have pleasurable experiences in life, but it means that you have them after you have done the hard and necessary work and completed your key tasks.

The payoff for practicing self-discipline is immediate. When you discipline yourself and force yourself to do the right thing, whether you feel like it or not, you like and respect yourself more. Your self-esteem increases, your self-image improves, your brain releases endorphins that make you feel happy and proud.

You actually get a payoff every time you hold your own feet to the fire.

The best part is that self-discipline is a habit that you can learn with practice and repetition. As I've pointed out, it takes approximately twenty-one days of repetition, without exception, to develop a habit of medium complexity. Sometimes you can develop a habit faster; sometimes it will take longer. It depends on you and how determined you are.

Some years ago, a businessman named Herbert Gray began searching for what he called the common denominator of success. He interviewed successful people over eleven years and finally concluded that successful people are those who make a habit of doing the things that unsuccessful people don't like to do. It turns out that successful people don't like to do them either, but they do them anyway, because they realize that they are the price of success.

Rich DeVos, the cofounder of Amway, once said, "There are lots of things in life that you don't like to do, like prospecting, selling, and building your business in the evenings and weekends, but you do them anyway, so that you can do the things that you really enjoy later on."

Every exercise of self-discipline strengthens every other positive quality at the same time, just as every weakness in self-discipline weakens you in other areas as well.

Nine Disciplines

There are nine disciplines you can develop that will improve every area of your life.

The first is the discipline of *clear thinking*. Thomas Edison once said that thinking is the hardest discipline of all, which is why so few people do it. It has been said that there are three types of people: those who think (a small minority), those who think they think, and those who would rather die than think.

Take some time to think through the critical issues and problems in your life today. Put aside long, unbroken chunks of time: thirty, sixty, and even ninety minutes. Peter Drucker said, "Fast people decisions are usually wrong people decisions." Fast decisions with regard to your family, career, money, or any other major issue are usually wrong decisions as well. Sit quietly for thirty or sixty minutes and think. Aristotle once said, "Wisdom, the ability to make good decisions, is a combination of experience plus reflection." The more time you take to think about your experiences, the more vital lessons you will gain from them.

Practice solitude on a regular basis. Go into the silence. Whenever you practice solitude for thirty minutes or more, you activate your superconscious mind and trigger your intuition. You get an answer from the still, small voice within.

To think better, take a pad of paper and write down every detail of the problem you are facing. Sometimes the right thing to do emerges as you write down the details.

Another way to think more clearly is to go for a walk or exercise for thirty to sixty minutes. Very often when you are exercising, you will get insights or ideas to help you to think better and make better decisions.

You can also talk your situation over with someone else whom you like and trust and who is not emotionally involved. Very often, a different perspective can totally change your viewpoint.

Always ask, what are my assumptions? What are you assuming about the situation? Alec Mackenzie, the time management specialist, once wrote, "Errant assumptions lie at the root of every failure."

What are your assumptions? What are you assuming to be true? What if your assumptions are wrong? What if you are proceeding on the basis of false information? Always be open to the possibility that you could be completely wrong in your current course of action. Be open to doing something completely different. Be open to the possibility that you don't have all the facts or you don't have the correct facts.

Daily Goal Setting

The second discipline that will make your success is *daily goal setting*. This alone has transformed my life, and the lives of thousands of other people.

You know that focus and concentration are the essential qualities for success. Start by asking, what do I really want to do with my life? Ask this question over and over until you get a clear answer. Imagine that you had $20 million in cash but only ten years to live. What would you immediately do differently in your life? Imagine that you have no limitations. Imagine that you could wave a magic wand and have all the time, money, education, experience, and contacts you need to achieve any goal. What would you do then?

Now here's the key: buy a spiral notebook and write in it every day. Write out ten goals in the PPP form: present, positive, and personal. Begin each goal with the word *I* followed by an action verb. For example, you could write, "I earn X number of dollars by this particular date."

Every day, before you start off, rewrite your top ten goals in the present tense as though you had already achieved them and you were reporting on this success to someone else.

Rewrite your goals on a clean page, without looking back to the previous page. Rewrite them from memory. Watch how your goals grow develop and change over time as you rewrite them each day. Many people have said that this discipline of daily goal setting has transformed their lives much faster than they had ever imagined.

Once I was giving a talk in Galveston, Texas. The man who introduced me stood up and said, "I have to tell you about my experience with Brian Tracy." Holding up a tattered spiral notebook, he said, "When I first met Brian, he told me to write down my goals every day. I started doing that. It changed my life completely." He waved his notebook and said, "I achieved every goal I ever wrote down. I've never seen anything more powerful in my whole life." You can do this yourself. It's a great discipline.

Daily Time Management

The third discipline is *daily time management*. Every minute spent in planning saves 10 minutes in execution. The more you plan, the better you use your time, and the more you accomplish. Imagine this: if you were to spend 10 to 12 minutes each morning to plan a day (which is all it takes), you will save 120 minutes, or 2 hours each day, in accomplishing your goals. That's a 25 percent increase in productivity from the simple act of planning your day in advance.

Begin by making a list of everything that you will do. The best time to write your daily list is the night before so that your subconscious can work on it while you sleep. Organize the list by priority before starting work. Go through and look at all the things you have to do, and pick what's most important and what's less important.

Practice the 80–20 rule, which says that 80 percent of your results come from 20 percent of your activities. What are those most valuable activities? Use the ABCDE method to set priorities, which, as we've seen, is based on considering the consequences of doing or not doing a particular task.

To recapitulate: An A task is something you must do: there are serious consequences for noncompletion. A B task is something you should do: there are only mild consequences for noncompletion. A C task is something nice to do, but it doesn't matter whether you do it or not. A D task is something that you delegate (and you delegate everything possible). An E task is something that you eliminate (and you eliminate everything you can to free up more time).

Once you've written ABCDE next to your tasks, go through and organize your list by A-1, A-2, A-3, and then B-1, B-2, B-3, and so on. Start on your A-1 task first thing in the morning. Once you start on your A-1 task, discipline yourself to concentrate single-mindedly on it until it's 100 percent complete.

The discipline of good time management spreads to all other forms of self-discipline. It has immediate payoff in improved results and long-term payoff in the quality of your life and work.

Courage

The fourth discipline is *courage*. Courage requires that you make yourself do what you should do; you deal with your fears rather than avoiding or running away from them. As I've already pointed out, the biggest obstacle to success is the fear of failure, expressed in the feeling *I can't, I can't*.

Courage is a habit developed by practicing it whenever it is required. As Emerson said, "Do the thing you fear, and the death of fear is certain." Make a habit of confronting your fears rather than avoiding them. When you confront the fear and move toward it—especially if it's another person, or people, or situation—the fear diminishes, and you become braver and more courageous. Actor Glenn Ford once said, "If you do not do the thing you fear, the fear controls your life." Repeat the words *I can do it, I can do it* over and over again to build up your courage and confidence. These words cancel out fears.

You begin to develop the habit of courage when you identify one fear in your life and discipline yourself to deal with it, to confront it, to do whatever is required as quickly as you possibly can.

The payoff for identifying and confronting a fear is tremendous. It gives you the courage and confidence to go through your life and deal with other fear inducing situations. Remember, the more you practice courage, the more you develop the habit of being completely unafraid.

Excellent Health Habits

The fifth discipline for success is *excellent health habits*. Your goal should be to live to be a hundred in superb physical health. Design and imagine your ideal body. What would your body look like if it was perfect in every way? This becomes your goal.

The key to health and fitness can be summarized in five words: *eat less, and exercise more*. Develop the discipline of exercising every day, even if all you do is go for a walk. Exercise is best done in the morning immediately after you get up, before you have time to think about it. Get up and get going. If you do this for twenty-one days, it will become part of your regular routine for the rest of your life.

Personally, I put my exercise clothes right next to my bed. When I get up, I virtually step on them. I put them on and start moving before I have a chance to think about it. Try it yourself.

Here's another key to excellent health habits: eliminate the three white poisons: flour, sugar, and salt. Recently I met a gentleman whom I've known for years. He'd lost thirty pounds, and his clothes were hanging on him like a loose tent. I said, "Good grief! How did you lose all the weight?" He said, "I stopped eating the three white poisons that you've been talking about for years."

I got a letter from a gentleman in Florida not long ago. He had become very successful in his business. He was very happy except for one thing: he was about thirty, and he was twenty-five pounds overweight. It was hurting his self-image. It made him unattractive to members of the opposite sex, and it really bothered him. Then he listened to a program of mine in which I mentioned the three white poisons. He said that made sense and cut out those things. Over the next six months, he dropped the twenty-five pounds and never put the weight on again. His self-concept changed; his self-image improved. He felt more attractive to other people. He said that just eliminating those white poisons changed his life forever.

Simply eliminating the white poisons will cause your weight to decline dramatically. It means that you stop eating any product that has flour in it: no breads, no pastries, no pastas. Eliminate anything with sugar: no soft drinks, no desserts, no pastries, no pop. Finally, eliminate salt. Never put salt on anything. Virtually everything you eat has too much salt on it already.

Does it take discipline? Of course it does. How do you do it? Eat more salads and other lighter foods. You can stuff your face with salads if you like without gaining weight, because salad is about 90 percent water, and it fills your stomach to the brim. Just make a habit of starting to eat more salads, and eat lighter foods. Instead of heavy steaks, eat fish, which is a much lighter food, digests much more rapidly, and gives you a tremendous amount of protein and nourishment.

Eat before 6 p.m., and eat half portions. My wife and I have begun a little ritual we call "salads at six." Instead of eating later in the evening, we strive to eat salad at six o'clock, because you don't need to eat very much in the evening. You want to eat at least three hours before you go to sleep. Just eat a salad at six. If you develop this habit, you'll be astonished at how light you feel, how well you sleep, how much weight you lose, and many other good things.

Another way to live to be a hundred is to get regular medical and dental checkups. One day my good friend Harvey Mackay asked me, "Have you had a medical checkup lately?"

I said, "No, I went a few years ago, but I'm in great shape."

"Brian," he said, "I just had a medical checkup, and I found something that they were able to take care of immediately. If I'd waited five years before going back, they'd have had to arrange for my funeral."

Regular medical checkups will add eight to ten years to your life, because doctors today can find possibly fatal conditions years in advance and eliminate them quickly. I've had a full medical checkup every year since getting that advice, and you should do the same thing.

Have you had your teeth checked on a regular basis? There's a close correlation between teeth health, gum health, and longevity. Take really good care of your teeth.

Use the Michael Jordan method when it comes to health habits: just do it. Just get on with it instead of procrastinating. Remember, you're the most precious person in your entire world. Take really good care of yourself.

Saving and Investing

The sixth discipline that will help you is *regular saving and investing*, which I've already covered. Resolve today to get out of debt, stay out of debt, and become financially independent. Make a decision to do it. No more wishing and hoping and praying; just get on with it. Your goal (and everyone's) is to achieve financial independence as soon as possible in life. This requires continual financial discipline with every dollar you earn. Again, the key is for you to save 10, 15, or even 20 percent of your income throughout your life. If you're in debt already, begin by saving 1 percent of your income, and then discipline yourself to live on the other 99 percent until this becomes a habit. Increase the amount of monthly savings to 2 or 3 percent and to 10 percent or percent. Discipline yourself to live on the balance.

The way you do this, by the way, is to go down to the bank and open a new bank account—your financial freedom account. Every day, when you come home, take your extra change and cash and put it in a jar on your dresser or in the kitchen. Let's say that you earn $3,000 a month. Well, 1 percent of that is $30. Every day you put $1 into the jar. At the end of each month, put the money into the account. Every time you get some spare cash, put it in the account. Every time you get a rebate or a discount or a check, put it in the account. Just keep throwing all your extra money into that account and letting it grow. Amazingly, it will start to grow far faster than you can imagine today. It begins with opening the account and putting something in to get it started.

It's critical to rewire your thinking from *I enjoy spending* to *I enjoy saving*. When you were a child and you received money, the first thing you probably did was to go out and buy candy. As an adult, you are still conditioned by that childhood response. When you receive money, you think of going out and buying adult candy: going on a trip, buying clothes, getting a car, going to a restaurant.

When you ask most people, "What would you do if you got a whole pile of money?" they say, "Oh, I'd go here and do that. I'd spend this and I buy that." Their first reaction is to blow the money.

So change your thinking from *I like spending* to *I love saving. I love putting money away. I love looking at that money growing and accumulating every month.* Pretty soon you change your whole mindset, and you start to think like financially successful people.

Delay and defer major purchases for thirty days or more. As I've already emphasized, sometimes when you put off a purchase that you were really keen on, you lose interest in buying it at all.

Investigate before you invest. Two thirds of investment success comes from avoiding mistakes. Invest as much time in studying the investment as you invested to earn the money in the first place. Every wealthy person I've known over the years does their due diligence. They study every single aspect and representation of an investment before they put a penny into it. They drag it out, they run it past their accountants, and they make sure that everything is correct. This doesn't guarantee that it will be successful, but it dramatically lowers the likelihood of making a mistake.

Pay cash for as many things as possible. Get rid of your credit cards. When you pay cash, the amount you're spending is far more visible and painful. Many young people get into debt today because they get credit cards in the mail. They look upon them as free money; it's not real cash until the bills come home.

One friend of mine got into serious financial trouble. He had zero interest on his credit card for the first month. The second month, it was 31 percent plus penalties.

I was listening to a financial expert the other day. She said, "If you have a $2,000 debt on your credit card, and you make the minimum payment, and it continues to grow at 24 to 31 percent interest, it will take you nine years to pay it off." Nine years.

People have no idea how serious credit card debt can be.

Remember what W. Clement Stone said: "If you cannot save money, the seeds of greatness are not in you." If you can, you can accomplish remarkable things in your financial life.

Hard Work

The seventh discipline is *hard work*. Your goal is to develop a reputation for being a hard worker. As Thomas Jefferson said, "The harder you work, the luckier you get."

The average work week in America, they say, is forty hours. Actually it's thirty-two hours. Why is that? Because people are at work officially for eight hours but they have one hour or more off for lunch and coffee breaks. Furthermore, the average person wastes 50 percent of the work day in idle chitchatting with coworkers, extended coffee breaks and luncheons, personal business, reading the newspaper, and surfing the Internet.

Here's the rule for success: work all the time you work. When you go to work, work. Imagine that this is work time: this is not playtime, this is not school time, this is not social time. Put your head down, go to work, and work all day long. If you do this, you will double your productivity, performance, and output. You will double your income, and you will become financially successful.

To lengthen your workday, start one hour earlier and immediately get to work. If you come in one hour earlier, you beat all the traffic, and you'll have one full hour to get your day started, to get your critical jobs under control, to make your phone calls, to make your plans because there's nobody there to interrupt you. Then work through your lunch hour, all day long; don't waste time.

Most people think about work as an extension of school, where you talk to your friends, hang around in class, have lunch, drink coffee, and socialize afterwards. No, no: work time is work time, and the better you do your work, the greater control you'll have over your life.

Work one hour later. Be the last to leave. Use this time after everybody goes to wrap up all your work and to plan your next day. I went to work once for a large conglomerate headed by a chairman who worked very hard. At five o'clock, the place cleared out as though there was a bomb scare. I kept on working till 5:30 or 6. One day I went down the hallway and found that he was the only other person working—the head of a $800 million conglomerate. I went in and asked him, "How's everything going?"

"Great."

"Is there any way I can be of service to you?"

He said, "I have this task, and I don't have time to take care of it. Could you do it for me?"

I said, "Sure." I took it and did it immediately.

The next day I went down the hallway, and the chairman was still there; we sat and chatted. Over the next year, I would go down and spend thirty to sixty minutes at the end of each day with him; each time he gave me new responsibilities. Before the dust settled, I was running three divisions, I had sixty-five people under my control, and I was being paid five times what I'd started earning a year before. My whole life changed when I started to work as hard as the big guy. It's really important to be the last to leave. You'll find that all your top people are still there, doing their extra work as well.

Three extra hours of work: start an extra hour early, work through lunch, and work an extra hour later. This will translate into six to eight hours of additional productivity. It will make you the most productive person in your company. Keep asking, what is the most valuable use of my time right now? Whatever your answer is, work on that every hour of every day. As your priorities change, of course that answer will shift. Work on what is now the most valuable use of your time.

What is the greatest time waster in the world of work? Other people. Other people want to talk; they don't have much going on in their lives, so they want to have a little chat with you. If somebody comes in or interrupts you, you have to say to them, "Thanks for coming in, but I've got to get back to work." Become known as the person in the company who's always got to get back to work, and people will stop bothering you and taking up your time.

Continual Learning

Discipline number eight is *continual learning*. Remember, to earn more, you must learn more. Jim Rohn is famous for saying, "Work at least as hard on yourself as you do on your work." Read in your field thirty to sixty minutes each day. This will translate into one book per week, fifty books per year. Listen to audio programs in your car as you drive from place to place: this will amount to an additional five hundred to a thousand hours per year.

Attend seminars, and take courses given by experts in your field. One idea from one course can save you years of hard work.

Persistence = Self-Discipline

The greatest test of self-discipline is persistence in the face of adversity: you drive yourself forward to complete your tasks 100 percent, no matter how you feel.

Courage has two parts. The first part is the courage to begin, to start, to launch forward with no guarantee of success. The second part is the courage to endure, to persist when you feel discouraged and tired and want to quit. Your persistence is your measure of your belief in yourself and your ability to succeed. The more you believe in the goodness and rightness of what you are doing, the more you persist. The more you persist, the more you tend to believe in yourself and in what you're doing.

These principles are reversible. Persistence is actually self-discipline in action. You demonstrate your self-discipline when you persist, even though you feel like quitting or giving up. Self-discipline leads to self-esteem, a greater sense of personal power, which leads to greater persistence, which leads to even greater self-discipline in an upward spiral.

Napoleon Hill said, "Persistence is to the character of man or woman as carbon is to steel." You make yourself into a better, stronger person by persisting when you feel like quitting. You take complete control over the development of your own character. Eventually, you become unstoppable.

The Benefits

The benefits of practicing self-discipline in every area of your life are many. Here are some of them:

1. The habit of self-discipline virtually guarantees your success in life, both with yourself and with others.

2. You'll get more done faster and have higher quality with discipline than with any other skill.

3. You will be paid more and promoted faster wherever you go.

4. You will experience a greater sense of self control, self-reliance, and personal power.

5. Self-discipline is the key to self-esteem, self-respect, and personal pride.

6. The greater your self-discipline, the greater your self-confidence, and the lower your fear of failure and rejection will be; nothing will stop you.

7. With self-discipline, you will have the strength of character to persist through all obstacles until you succeed.

Begin today to practice self-discipline in every area of your life. Persistently practice until it comes to you as automatically as breathing in and breathing out. When you become a completely self-disciplined person, your future will be guaranteed.

11

The Challenge Response

Sometimes it seems that problems are the number one fact of life. No sooner is one solved than another appears to take its place. The process seems endless, and in all practical respects, it probably is. No matter who they are or what they do, every person experiences problems, difficulties, unexpected reversals, and crises that knock them off balance and often threaten their very survival. That's why problem-solving is one of the most important skills you need to gain for success.

It's estimated that every business has a crisis every two to three months that, if not dealt with quickly and effectively, can threaten its survival. Similarly, each individual has a crisis—it may have to do with personal, financial, family, or health matters—every two or three months. When the going gets tough, the tough get going. It is only in crunch time that you demonstrate to yourself and others what you are really made of. As the Greek philosopher Epictetus once said, "Circumstances do not make the man. They merely reveal him to himself and to others as well."

Between 1934 and 1961, historian Arnold Toynbee wrote his twelve-volume series, *A Study of History*, in which he examined the rise and fall of twenty-six civilizations over three thousand years. Much of what he discovered in the life cycles of those empires applies to the rise and fall of businesses and industries, large and small, and to individuals as well.

Toynbee found that every civilization began as a small tribe or group of people that was suddenly faced with a challenge from the outside, usually an attack from hostile tribes. To deal with this external threat, the leader had to immediately reorganize and respond effectively in order to survive. If the leader made the right decisions and took the right actions, the tribe would rise to the challenge, defeat the enemy, and in the process grow and become stronger. In growing stronger, the tribe would bump into or trigger confrontation with another, larger hostile tribe, thereby creating another challenge. As long as the leaders and the tribe continued to rise to overcome the inevitable challenges confronting them, they would continue to survive and grow. Toynbee also found that civilizations continued to grow as long as they met the challenges that they were facing from the outside, and every civilization began to decline when it could no longer do so. Toynbee called this the *challenge response theory of civilization.*

These principles apply to your personal life as well. From the time you start in business, you will be confronted with problems, difficulties, failures, and challenges of all kinds. No sooner will you solve one problem than you'll be confronted with another, often larger and more complicated. Your personal level of responsibility determines your survival, success, health, happiness, and prosperity. Everything is contained in your response.

Toynbee also found that the challenges came unbidden. Nobody could anticipate them or prepare for them: the only part of the equation they could control was the response to the challenge.

Everything was in the response.

It is not what happens to you, but how you deal with it that counts. The only way to realize your full potential and become everything you are capable of becoming is by dealing effectively with crunch time. The only way to achieve all your goals is by responding effectively to the inevitable crisis of day-to-day life.

The good news is that right now, you have within you everything you need to deal with any problem or crisis you will ever face. There's no problem that you cannot solve by applying your intelligence and creativity to finding a solution. There's no obstacle that you cannot overcome or get around if you are determined and persistent enough.

Stay Calm

The first rule for surviving and thriving at crunch time is to *stay calm*. When you experience a sudden setback or reversal, your first job is to seize control of your thoughts and feelings and make sure to perform at your best. When things go wrong, the natural tendency is to overreact or react in a negative way. You can become angry or upset or afraid. The stressful thoughts and negative emotions immediately start to shut down major parts of your brain, including your neocortex—the thinking part of your brain—which you use to analyze, assess, solve problems, and make decisions.

If you don't consciously and immediately assert mental and emotional control when things go wrong, you will automatically resort to the fight-or-flight reaction. You will start to react emotionally, because you won't have the capacity to think calmly and clearly.

The starting point of staying calm in a crisis is to refuse to react automatically and unthinkingly. Imagine that every situation is a test to see what you're truly made of. Imagine that everyone is watching and waiting to see how you will respond. You can keep yourself calm by resolving to set a good example, be a role model for others, and demonstrate the correct way to deal with a major problem, as if you were giving a lesson. Remember, your response to the crisis is everything. This is the test.

The primary source of negative emotions is frustrated expectations: you expected a thing to happen in a particular way, but something altogether different has happened. The two major forms of negative emotion are triggered: our old enemies, the fear of failure and the fear of rejection. Either of them can cause anger, depression, or even paralysis.

You experience the fear of failure when you're dealing with the potential loss of money, customers, position, reputation, or the life and well-being of another person. You experience the fear of rejection (which is closely associated with fears of criticism and disapproval) when something goes wrong and you feel as if you are not capable or competent, or that others will think poorly of you.

Your thoughts, emotions, and actions are largely determined by your explanatory style: the way you explain or interpret things to yourself. Fully 95 percent of your emotions, positive or negative, are caused by the way you interpret the things that are happening around you. Although your mind can hold thousands of thoughts in a row, it can only hold one thought at a time. You're always free to choose that thought at any moment.

Here's an example: instead of using the word *problem* or *crisis*, simply use the word *situation*. A problem is negative, but a situation is neutral. You say, "We are facing an interesting situation here." That keeps you and everybody calm.

Even better, use the word *challenge*: "This is an interesting challenge that we hadn't expected." Or, even better, use "This is an opportunity" to describe a setback or difficulty. Using these words keeps your mind positive and creative, and also keeps you in complete control.

Stay calm by refusing to catastrophize. Few things are ever as bad as they seem initially. Ask questions of the others involved, and listen patiently to the answers. Talking over the problem with a spouse or a trusted friend can help immensely to keep you calm and controlled.

Within every problem you face is the seed of an equal or greater benefit or advantage. When you discipline yourself to look for the good in a situation and seek the valuable lessons that it might contain, you automatically remain calm, positive, and optimistic.

Remain Confident

Another key to mastering difficult situations is to remain confident in your abilities. The natural reaction to an unexpected reversal is to feel stunned, shocked, and angry, as if you had just been punched in the emotional solar plexus. Although this is normal, remember that you have the ability to rise to any challenge.

Talk to yourself positively. To rebuild your self-confidence, say things like *I like myself, I can handle anything,* or *I can handle anything that comes along.* You can neutralize the negative feelings triggered by the fear of failure by repeating over and over to yourself, *I can do it, I can do this, I can take care of this.* Talk to yourself in a positive way. Tell yourself that you can do anything that you put your mind to. Tell yourself that there is no problem that you cannot solve.

The Worry Buster Formula

There's a wonderful way to deal with any crisis or problem, and it's called the *worry buster formula.* Use it in every situation. It consists of four parts:

1. Define the problem clearly, preferably in writing. Most problems can be solved if they are clearly defined at first. Remember, in medicine, they say accurate diagnosis is half the cure.

When we have a challenge in our company, I'll often sit people down and ask, "All right, what exactly is the situation?" We will write it on a flip chart or a whiteboard. As we do, people say, "Well, no, it's not exactly that. What about this?" We will keep writing it out until the situation is clearly described; once it is, in 50 percent of cases there's an obvious solution, and we're back to work.

2. Ask yourself, what is the worst possible outcome of this problem? What is the worst thing that can happen? Look at everything: you could lose your money, your time, your customer, your business. Identify the worst thing that can happen, clearly and honestly.

3. Resolve to accept the worst should it occur. Say, "All right, if this occurs, it won't kill me." Once you've decided to accept the worst, your mind becomes clear and calm. You can begin thinking about the future, because all of your stress is gone.

4. Begin immediately to improve upon the worst. Begin immediately to make sure that the worst doesn't happen. What can you do right now to resolve this situation? Whatever it is, concentrate single-mindedly on reducing the worst possible consequences, and you're back in complete mental control of the situation. The only real antidote to worry is purposeful action in the direction of your goals.

Self-confidence and self-esteem come from a feeling of forward motion toward your goals. Get so busy working on the solutions to your problems that you don't have time to worry about what has happened, especially things that you cannot change. Then move forward.

Qualities of Leaders

The most common quality of leaders throughout the ages is *vision*. Leaders have a clear, exciting vision of where they want to go and what they want to accomplish in the future.

The second most common quality of leaders is *courage*. The fact is that everyone is afraid. We all have fears of different kinds, small and large, hidden and exposed. As Mark Twain said, "Courage is resistance to fear, mastery of fear—not absence of fear."

The worst effect of the fear of failure is that it can cause paralysis. People go into a state of emotional shock. Emerson once wrote, "If you would become a success, you must resolve to confront your fears. If you do the thing you fear, the death of fear is certain." You develop courage in yourself by facing your fears and doing the things that you are most afraid to do.

In business and in personal life, the most prevalent fear is the fear of confrontation. You have to develop the courage to confront the difficult people in your life and to resolve the situation. Fortunately, you can develop courage by acting courageously. When you do something you fear, you feel more courageous.

In life, the courage follows the courageous behavior. As Emerson wrote, "Do the thing, and you will have the power." An old man once said to his grandson, "Act boldly, and unseen forces will come to your aid." Author Dorothea Brande once wrote that the most important advice she ever received was this: "Act as if it were impossible to fail, and it shall be."

The Reality Principle

Jack Welch, the late president of General Electric, said that the most important of all leadership principles was the reality principle: facing the world as it is rather than as you wish it would be. In any difficult situation, begin by asking, what's the reality?

Harold Geneen, the executive who built ITT into a $560 billion international conglomerate, said that the most important element to solving problems is to get the facts. You must get the real facts, he said, not the alleged facts, the assumed facts, the hoped-for facts, or the imagined facts. If something has happened, especially if it is a past event that cannot be changed, it falls into the categories of facts.

Whenever you face crunch time in your life or business, call time-out and focus on getting all the information you can. Ask questions, and listen carefully to the answers. What is the situation exactly? What has happened? How did it happen? When did it happen? Where did it happen? What are the facts? How do we know they are accurate? Who is involved? Who is responsible for doing or not doing certain things? Never worry or become upset about a fact, about something you cannot change.

Resist the temptation to become angry or blame others for their mistakes and shortcomings. Refuse to blame anyone for anything. As soon as you stop blaming other people and take responsibility for the future, your negative emotions cease, your mind becomes calm and clear, and you begin to make better decisions. Focus instead on understanding the situation and determining the specific actions.

Two of the best questions you can ask in any crisis are, what are we trying to do, and how are we trying to do it? What are our assumptions in this situation? What if our assumptions are wrong? If we were wrong in one of our major assumptions, what would that mean? What would we have to do differently? Never assume that you have all the information or that the information you have is correct.

Do not confuse correlation with causation. Most people tend to jump to conclusions too quickly. In many cases when two events happen at the same time, people assume that one event is the cause of the other. Very often, however, two events occur simultaneously, yet neither event has anything to do with the other. Assuming a causal link between the two can lead to confusion and poor decision making. Don't let this happen to you.

Take Control of Your Mind

When things go wrong, you will tend to respond with negativity, fear, and anger. Whenever you feel hurt or threatened by loss or criticism, you react to protect yourself with the fight-or-flight response. As a leader, however, your first job is to take firm control over your mind and emotions, and then to take control over the situation—in that order.

Leaders focus on the future, not the past. They focus on what can be done now to resolve the problem or improve the situation. They focus on what is under their control and on their next decisions and actions, and you must do the same.

When a company gets into serious trouble, the board will often fire the existing president and bring in a turn-around specialist, who immediately takes complete control of the organization. He centralizes all decision making in his office. He takes control of all expenditures, right down to signing every check, so that he knows exactly what monies are going out of the company, and to whom. He then acts boldly and often ruthlessly, making whatever hard decisions are required, and doing whatever is necessary to save the company.

To be your own turnaround specialist, the first thing you must do is, again, to accept 100 percent responsibility for yourself and everything that happens from this moment forward. Leaders accept responsibility and take charge. Non-leaders avoid responsibility and pass things off on to others. You must especially keep yourself positive and focused. You do this by reminding yourself with these words: *I am responsible, I am responsible*. Or as Harry Truman said, "The buck stops here. I'm the one in charge." Say to yourself, *if it's to be, it's up to me*.

The Six Stages of Grief

The psychologist Elisabeth Kübler-Ross described the stages that a person goes through in facing death (either of a loved one or of oneself, as with a terminal diagnosis). She identified five stages of grief: denial, anger, blame, depression, and acceptance. For life crises, we can add a sixth stage: *resurgence*, or taking control.

Your first reaction to a major setback will often be denial: you will be shocked and feel that this cannot be happening. Your first reaction will be to shut it out and hope that it's not true.

The second stage in dealing with a major setback is anger. You will tend to lash out at those you feel are responsible for your problem.

The third stage of dealing with death or disappointment is blame. In business, it's quite common for a witch hunt to begin to determine who exactly is to blame and for what. This behavior satisfies the deep need in many people to find someone guilty whenever something goes wrong.

The fourth stage in dealing with disappointment is depression. The reality sets in: an unavoidable and irreparable setback has occurred, the damage has been done, and money has been lost. Depression is often accompanied by feelings of self-pity, of being a victim. You often feel let down, cheated, or betrayed by others; you feel sorry for yourself.

The fifth stage of dealing with difficulties is acceptance. You finally reach the stage where you realize that the crisis has happened and that it is irreversible, like a broken dish or spilled milk. You come to terms with the loss and begin to look toward the future.

The final stage in dealing with a major setback is resurgence. You take complete control of yourself in the situation and begin thinking about what you can do next to solve the problem and move forward.

Everyone goes through the first five stages; it's quite normal and natural. The only question is, how quickly do you go through them? The mark of mentally healthy individuals is their resilience in response to the inevitable ups and downs of life. As Charlie Jones, the great speaker, said, "It's not how far you fall, but how high you bounce that counts." Recognize that everyone makes mistakes. Things go wrong all the time. Even the best and most competent people do foolish things occasionally, as do you.

If someone else has dropped the ball, instead of being angry or punishing, treat the person with kindness and compassion. Always try to assume the best intentions on everyone's part, and then focus on solving the problem and taking action.

Creative Abandonment

According to the Managers Institute, the most important quality necessary for success in business in the twenty-first century is flexibility. With the explosion in knowledge and technology, combined with a rapid growth of competition, products, services, processes, markets, and customers, changes are taking place at a more rapid rate today than ever before.

Perhaps the most important tool that you can use to remain flexible and adaptable in turbulent times is *zero-based thinking*. You stop, stand back, and look at your business objectively, as though you were an outsider looking in. You ask this question: is there anything that I am doing today that, knowing what I now know, that I wouldn't do if I were starting up again? Discipline your-self to ask and answer this question honestly on a regular basis. Whenever you do, you see things in a different light. Is there any product or service that, knowing what you now know, you would not offer or bring to the market today if you had to do it again? If there is, your next question must be, how do I discontinue this product or service, and how fast?

Peter Drucker calls this the *process of creative abandonment*. You must be prepared to abandon any product or service that is draining time and resources away from the sale and delivery of more popular and profitable products and services. Is there any activity or business process that, knowing what you now know, you wouldn't start up again today? Is there any expense, method, or procedure in your business operations that, knowing what you now know, you wouldn't start again? Is there any person in your business who you would not hire today, knowing what you now know? Is there anyone in your business who you would not promote, assign, or give a particular responsibility to, knowing what you now know?

On a personal level, is there any relationship or situation in your personal life that, knowing what you now know, you wouldn't get into again today, if you could do it all over?

Another way to cut your losses is to imagine that you arrive at work one morning to find that your entire business has burned to the ground. Fortunately, your staff is safe and standing around in the parking lot, watching the building as it was consumed in flames. As it happens, there are offices available across the street that you could move into immediately and restart your business.

If this happened to you, what products and services would you immediately start producing for sale? What customers would you contact immediately? What business activities would you engage in first? Most importantly, what business activities, processes, and expenses would you *not* get into again today if you were starting over?

If ever you should downsize, discontinue, or eliminate anything or anyone to save your business, you should do it immediately at crunch time. Don't delay: cut off all nonessential expenses and eliminate all nonessential activities. Get back to basics. Focus on the 20 percent of your products, services, and people that account for most of your results.

Four Steps for Managing a Crisis

As I've said, in a turbulent, fast-changing, highly competitive environment, you will have a crisis of some kind every two or three months—a business crisis, a financial crisis, a family crisis and personal crisis, or even a health crisis. This is the critical moment in your business or life. This is the testing time. Whatever you do or fail to do can be extraordinarily important. It can have significant consequences, positive or negative, on the future of your business or your life.

When a crisis occurs, there are four things that you should do immediately.

1. Stop the bleeding. Practice damage control; put every possible limitation on losses. In business, you must preserve cash at all costs.

2. Gather information. Get the facts, speak to the key people, and find out exactly what you're dealing with.

3. Discipline yourself to think only in terms of solutions: what you can do immediately to minimize the damage and solve the problems.

4. Become action-oriented. Think in terms of your next step. Often any decision is better than no decision at all.

Crisis Anticipation

One key strategy for business and personal success is called *crisis anticipation*. You practice crisis anticipation by looking ahead into the future three, six, nine, and twelve months and asking what could happen to disrupt your business and personal life. What are the worst possible things that could happen sometime in the future? Refuse to play games with your own mind; refuse to wish, hope, or pretend certain things could never happen to you. Develop an "if this happened, then what?" mentality. Even if there is only a small probability that something disastrous could occur, the superior thinker carefully considers all the possible consequences of that problem and provides accordingly. Develop a contingency plan for possible emergencies and crises.

What steps would you take if something went seriously wrong? What would you do first? What would you do second? How would you react? Look down the road into the future. Imagine what could happen, and then come back to the present to plan well in advance of the possible occurrence.

To ensure that the crisis does not repeat itself, do a debriefing. What exactly happened? How did it happen? What did we learn? What could we do to make sure it doesn't happen again? According to Stanford University, the most important quality of the top CEOs among the Fortune 1000 corporations was their ability to deal with a crisis.

How you manage the inevitable crisis is the true measure of your level of wisdom and maturity. Your ability to anticipate a crisis, and to learn from it, is essential to your ability to deal with subsequent crises when they occur.

Begin by identifying the three worst things that could happen in your business or financial life in the next year. What could you do today to minimize the damage from these crises? Identify the worst things that could happen in your personal and family life. Then take the steps to make sure that they don't happen. Apply zero-based thinking to every part of your business and personal life. Are you doing anything that you would not get into again today, knowing what you now know?

Imagine that you could start your personal or business life over again today. What would you get into? What would you get out of? What would you start up? What would you let go of?

Accept complete responsibility for the problem, take command, take charge, and get through the five stages of grief as quickly as possible. Refuse to blame anyone for anything, except to acknowledge that people make mistakes. Focus on the solution rather than on who did what and who is to blame.

Be your own consultant. Take any problem that you are facing today, imagine that you have been hired to analyze it thoroughly, and make recommendations for solutions to your client. Be calm and objective, as if you were an outside advisor. Determine the nature of the problem by getting all the relevant facts. Very often you don't have the right facts. Very often what appears to be a problem or crisis is not that serious at all, because you have only heard half the story. Once you hear the rest of the story, you realize that it's not that big a deal. Take the time to investigate thoroughly before you react.

Identify a person, situation, or action that you fear. Resolve to confront it immediately, and get it behind you. Make a habit throughout your life of doing the things you fear, and the death of fear is certain.

Whatever decisions you would make if your survival was at stake, make them now; don't delay. Your ability to deal effectively with the inevitable crises of daily life is the true mark of your character and personality.

The starting point of effectively dealing with crunch time is to visualize yourself as calm, cool, and collected in the face of any unexpected problem or reversal. See yourself in your mind's eye as if you are completely in charge of any situation. Then, when the situation arises unexpectedly, you will be mentally prepared to perform at your best.

Remember, there is no problem that you cannot solve, no obstacle that you cannot overcome, and no goal that you cannot achieve by applying your mind to your situation. Never give up.

12

Simplifying Your Life

Everyone today has too much to do and too little time. You feel overwhelmed with duties, tasks, and responsibilities. Your challenge is to simplify your life in such a way that you spend more time doing the things that are most important to you and less time doing those things that are not important at all. In this chapter, you will learn a variety of methods, techniques, and strategies for reorganizing and restructuring your life, simplifying your activities, getting more done, and enjoying more time with your family and in your personal life.

Determine Your Values

The starting point of simplifying your life is to decide exactly what is most important to you. What are your values? What are your core beliefs? What do you care about more than anything else? The most important question that you must ask and answer throughout your life is, what do I really want to do with my life? What you want to do with your life will invariably be an expression of what is called your irreducible essence, the person that you really are deep inside.

To simplify your life, set peace of mind as your highest goal, and then organize your life around it. Whatever gives you peace, satisfaction, joy, and the feeling of value and importance is right for you. Whatever causes you stress, distraction, unhappiness, or irritation is wrong for you. You must have the courage to organize your life so that you're doing more of the things that give you the greatest joy and satisfaction, and fewer of the things that take away from your joy and satisfaction.

Decide What You Want

In every study of unhappy people that I've ever read, I've found that they have one thing in common: they have no clear goals—no sense of direction. They have many wishes and hopes and desires, but they do not have goals to which they are committed. As a result, their lives go around in circles, leaving them feeling dissatisfied and empty most of the time.

Make a list of ten goals that you would like to achieve. Then ask, what one goal, if I achieved it in the next twenty-four hours, would have the greatest positive impact on my life? This goal usually leaps out at you from the page. Put a circle around it.

You are now ready to reorganize your life and simplify your activities. Your most important goal becomes your major, definite purpose, your focal point for the foreseeable future.

Make a list of everything you can think of that you can do to achieve that goal. Then begin immediately on the most important thing that you can do to achieve your most important goal.

Throughout the day, think about your goal. When you get up in the morning, think about your goal. When you go to bed at night, think about your goal. Do something every day that moves you toward the achievement of your most important goal. This action alone will simplify and streamline your life in ways that you cannot now imagine.

Get Your Life in Balance

The key to balance is to make sure that your activities on the outside are aligned with your values on the inside. You experience happiness, peace, joy, and relief when you return to your values and ensure that everything you do is consistent with them. On the other hand, most of your stress, unhappiness, negativity, and dissatisfaction comes from attempting to do things in your outer world that are in conflict with your most important values on the inside.

Use the 20–10 exercise: imagine that you have $20 million cash in the bank, tax-free. Imagine also that you only have 10 years left to live and to spend and enjoy this $20 million. What changes would you make in your life?

One important key to simplification is to imagine that you have no limits on anything that you would want to be, have, or do. Imagine that you have all the time and all the money you need. Imagine that you have all the skills and ability that you need. Imagine that you have all the friends and contacts that you require. Imagine that you could do anything that you wanted. What would it be?

"I Was Wrong"

As we saw in the previous chapter, with zero-based thinking, you draw a line under every decision or commitment you've ever made. You then ask this question: *knowing what I now know, is there anything that I am doing today that I would not start up again today, if I had to do it over?*

To simplify your life, you must be willing to admit that you are not perfect. Be prepared to say the magic words *I was wrong*. The sooner you admit this, the sooner you can simplify and improve your life. Be willing to say, *I made a mistake*. There's nothing wrong with this: it's how everyone learns and grows. What is wrong is refusing to correct the mistake because our ego is invested in being right. Psychologist Gerald Jampolsky once asked, "Do you want to be right, or do you want to be happy?" You have to make this decision for yourself.

Finally, learn to say regularly, *I've changed my mind*. It's amazing how many people dig themselves into holes of stress, anger, frustration, and dissatisfaction because they're not willing to admit that they've changed their mind.

This is not for you. You must stand back and look at your entire life. Is there anything in your life that you would not get into again today if you had to do it over? If there is, have the courage to admit that you have made a mistake—which all people do—and then take the steps to change.

Reorganize Your Activities

There are only four ways to change the quality of your life: You can do more of some things. You can do less of other things. You can start doing something that you're not doing today. You can stop doing something else. Apply one or more of these to every part of your life in order to simplify it.

Stand back and look at your life, especially the parts that are causing you stress and frustration. How could you reorganize those areas so that you're doing more and more of the things that give you the greatest happiness, and fewer and fewer of other things?

Reorganize your life so that you do more tasks of a similar nature at the same time. Start a little earlier, work a little harder, stay a little later, and do several similar tasks at once, rather than spreading them out. Continually think about how you could reorganize your life to make it simpler and better.

Restructure your work. Remember to apply the 80–20 rule to everything you do. Eighty percent of the value of everything you do will be contained in 20 percent of the actions that you take. This means that fully 80 percent of the things you do have little or no value. The secret to restructuring your work and your life is for you to spend more and more time doing the 20 percent of things that contribute the most to your life and work. Simultaneously, spend less and less time doing those things that contribute very little; sometimes you should stop doing them completely. The worst use of time is to do very well what need not be done at all.

Reengineer Your Personal Life

The whole process of reengineering is based on the exercise of reducing steps in any process. In business, we encourage people to make a list of all the steps in a particular work process; then we look for a way to reduce the number of steps by at least 30 percent the first time through. This is usually quite easy.

In your own life, there are three keys to reengineering your life, reducing steps, and simplifying your activities:

1. Delegate everything that you possibly can to other people. The more things of low value that you delegate, the more time you free up. The more time you'll have for the things that only you can do that make a real difference.

2. Outsource everything in your business that can be done by other companies that specialize in that activity. Most companies are bogged down in activities that other companies can do for them better and more efficiently, and usually at a lower price.

3. Eliminate all low-value and no-value activities. As Nancy Reagan said, "Just say no" to anything that is not the highest and best use of your time.

Reinvent Yourself Regularly

Imagine that your company, your job, and your career disappeared overnight and you had to start all over again. What would you do differently?

Imagine that you had to combine and recombine your education and experience into a new career or field of activity. What would you really love to do if you had all the skills, ability, and money that you needed? You should be reinventing yourself regularly, at least once each year. You should stand back and look at your life and career and ask yourself, *if I were not now doing this, knowing what I now know, would I get into it?* If the answer is no, your next question is, *how do I get out and how fast?*

Set Priorities

One of the best ways to simplify your life is to reorganize your priorities. Realize that fully 80 percent of the things you do have low or no value. By setting priorities, you focus more and more of your time on doing those few things that really make a difference in your life—the things that really make you happy.

The most important word in setting priorities is *consequences*. If something is important, the potential consequences of doing it or not doing it are high. If something is unimportant, the potential consequences of doing it or not doing it are low. Ask yourself every hour of every day, what can I and only I do that, if done well, will make a real difference? Whatever your answer is to this question, work on that above all others.

Set limits. The only way that you can simplify your life and get control of your time is by stopping doing certain things. You are already too busy. Your dance card is full. It is impossible for you to simplify your life merely by learning how to be more efficient and effective. You also have to stop doing as many things as possible.

In order to begin a new task, you must stop or discontinue an old task. In order to get into something new, you must get out of something old; you are already overworked. You cannot do more than you're already doing. Practice creative abandonment with tasks and activities that are no longer as important as others; instead do fewer and fewer things, but do things of higher value.

Plan Your Time

There's an old saying: proper prior planning prevents poor performance. It's called the six P formula. Every minute spent in planning saves ten to twelve minutes in execution. This means that you save as much as 90 percent of the time you need to get through the day by planning every step in advance; it is almost miraculous.

Plan your year in advance, especially vacations with your families and friends. Book them, pay for them, and take them off your calendar, exactly as if they were appointments with your biggest and most important customer.

Plan each month in advance: lay it out in front of you, and determine how you're going to spend the time. You will be amazed at how much more productive you are and how much simpler your life is by the act of planning your month in advance.

Plan every week in advance, preferably the weekend before. Sit down and plan every day, using the 70 percent rule. This rule says that you should commit yourself for no more than 70 percent of your time. Leave yourself some slack in your schedule so that you have time for unexpected emergencies and delays.

Plan each day in advance, preferably the night before. Make a list of everything you have to do, and organize it by priority. Select your A-1 task, and be ready to begin on that task first thing in the morning.

Delegate Everything Possible

When you start your career, you have to do everything yourself.

If you're going to grow, evolve, and become highly effective and well paid, you must delegate everything possible to anyone who can possibly do the task. Use your hourly rate as a measure. How much do you earn per hour? If you earn $50,000 per year, your hourly rate is approximately $25 per hour. Delegate everything to anyone who can do a task at a lower hourly rate than you hope to make. It is sometimes better to sit and do nothing, simply thinking and using your creative powers, than to do low-paid tasks that tire you out and consume your time.

When you delegate to other people, make sure that they have the proven ability to do it. Delegation is not abdication: once you have delegated a task, you must supervise it to make sure that it is done on time, on schedule, and on budget. Inspect what you expect.

Focus on higher-value tasks. Keep organizing and reorganizing your work so that you're spending more and more time on those few tasks have the highest possible value.

The most important time management question, which you should ask and answer every hour of every day, is, *what is the most valuable use of my time right now?* Whatever your answer to that question, be sure that you are working on it every minute of every day.

Work Single-Mindedly

Select your most important task—A-1 on your list—start on that task, and then discipline yourself to work on it single-mindedly until it's complete. Time management experts have found that if you start and stop a task several times, you can increase the amount of time necessary to complete it by as much as 500 percent. You can make it five times longer than necessary.

On the other hand, when you focus single-mindedly on a task, you can reduce the amount of time necessary to complete it by 80 percent. This gives you a 400 percent return on the investment of your time and energy. All that extra time then becomes available to you to do other things in your life that give you more joy and satisfaction.

Reduce Your Paperwork

Use the TRAF method to reduce your paperwork and get through large quantities of newspapers and magazines. T stands for *toss*. These are the things that you throw away immediately without reading them. This habit alone is a great time saver and simplifier. R stands for *refer*. These are things that you refer to other people to handle rather than bothering with them yourself. The third letter, A, stands for *action*. These are the things that you need to act on personally: you put these into a read file, and you work on them, organized by priority, throughout the day.

The last letter, F, stands for *file*. These are the things that have to be filed for later. Remember two things: Fully 80 percent of the things you file are never referred to again; they just clutter up your closets. Second, whenever you order something to be filed, you create work for and complicate the life of someone else. Don't do this unless it's absolutely essential.

Leave Things Off

Develop the habit of leaving your radio off when you travel, especially with your family and friends. When you come home at night, leave the television off. Whenever you leave the radio and television off, you create a sound vacuum, which is filled by conversation, interaction, and the true joys of family and personal life. Instead, use a TiVo system to record the programs that you like without commercials, so that you can watch them when you want, at your own convenience.

When you get up in the morning, resist the temptation to turn on the television. Instead, spend a few minutes reading something educational, motivational, or inspirational. Take some time to plan your day. Think about who you are and what you want rather than filling your mind with the noise of endless television or radio.

Put Relationships First

Most of the enjoyment and satisfaction that you get in life will come from your interactions with other people. Put the most important people in your life at the top of your priorities. Put everything else below these people.

Imagine that you only have six months left to live. What would you do? How would you spend your time? Whatever your answer to this, I'm sure it does not involve earning more money or getting back to the office to return phone calls.

How would you change your life if you had all the money that you wanted or needed? In almost every case, you would think about the things that you would do with the people that you care about the most. Don't wait until you are financially independent or have only six months to live before you start to spend more time with the most important people in your life. Do it now.

Take Care of Your Health

You can simplify your life by eating less and eating better, exercising regularly and getting thinner, getting regular medical and dental checkups, eating proper foods, and taking excellent care of yourself.

Imagine that you had become very rich, and you had bought a million-dollar racehorse. How would you feed that horse? I can promise you that you would not feed that horse with fast food, junk food, sodas, or potato chips. You would feed that horse with the finest foods you could find in the whole world.

Well, you are a thousand, times more valuable than a million-dollar racehorse. Feed yourself the same way you would feed a million-dollar horse. Take good care of your health.

Practice Solitude Daily

Take thirty to sixty minutes each day to sit in silence with yourself. Take the time to listen to yourself and your inner voice. The practice of solitude will transform your life. In solitude, you will get ideas and insights that can change everything you do. When you practice solitude on a regular basis, you will feel a great sense of calm, quiet creativity, and relaxation. You will emerge from your periods of solitude feeling wonderful about yourself and your life.

Solitude is one of the most wonderful joys available to the human being. It costs nothing except the discipline to sit quietly for thirty to sixty minutes by yourself on a regular basis. Give it a try.

The Goal of Life

You can simplify your life by practicing these ideas over and over until they become automatic and easy. Make it a habit to look for ways to do fewer things, but to do more important things. Make it a habit to simplify your life and simultaneously increase the joy and satisfaction that you receive.

Your goal is to live a long, happy life, full of joy and satisfaction, to realize your potential, and to become everything you are capable of becoming. Aristotle, perhaps the greatest philosopher of all time, determined that the ultimate aim of all human life and behavior is to achieve happiness. This is the primary purpose of all human activity. How, then, shall we live in order to be happy?

The starting point of achieving balance in your life is to set your own happiness as the primary goal of your life, and then organize everything you do to achieve that. If you accomplish everything in life, but you're not happy, you've failed to realize your full potential.

Fully 85 percent of your happiness comes from your relationships with other people, at home, at work, and in every area of your life. You require a balance between your work and your personal life in order to be happy.

Four Key Areas

There are four key areas of life that you need to balance against each other:

1. **Health, energy, and personal fitness.** You need to take sufficient time for health and fitness, eating the right foods, exercising, and getting enough rest.

2. **Family and relationships.** You need to spend ample time with the most important people in your life, doing the things that give you the greatest amount of joy and satisfaction.

3. **Work and career.** You need to be doing work that you enjoy, that gives you a sense of personal fulfillment, that pays you well, and that you do in an excellent fashion.

4. **Financial independence.** Get control of your finances, save and invest on a regular basis, and feel that you are moving step by step toward financial independence.

In addition, you need to be learning and growing, contributing to your community, and developing spiritually. If you're lacking in any of these areas, your life quickly goes out of balance. Stress occurs when what you are doing on the outside is inconsistent with what is truly important to you on the inside.

One of the most important questions you can ask in every part of your life, especially in making decisions, is *what is really important here?* Remember the 80–20 rule: 80 percent of your happiness and satisfaction will come from 20 percent of the things you do.

Your most important ability is your ability to think. The better you think, the better decisions you make. The better decisions you make, the better actions you take. The better actions you take, the better results you get in every area.

What is really working in your life? What parts of your life give you your greatest feelings of pleasure and satisfaction? What people and activities make you the happiest? What is not working? What is causing you stress, frustration, or unhappiness? The greater clarity you have in answering these two questions—*what's working?* and *what's not working?*—the faster you can achieve balance in your life. Human beings are creatures of habit. They often get into a routine or a comfort zone where they do certain things over and over, even though those things no longer work or make them happy.

A major source of stress in adult life is denial. Denial arises when we refuse to face the truth of an important part of our lives. Perhaps we are dissatisfied with our job. Perhaps a relationship is no longer right for us. Perhaps we've made a bad decision or life choice. Every act of denial puts your life out of balance, increases stress, and opens you up to psychosomatic illnesses like colds and flus of all kinds. Practice the reality principle. Insist upon seeing the world as it really is rather than the way that you would like it to be.

Never get upset about something that you can't change, and you can't change people, and you can't change past events. The opposite of denial is acceptance. When you accept that people and situations are the way they are and are not likely to change, the stress of denial begins to disappear.

Human beings are choosing organisms; we make choices. Every minute of every day, you make a choice between what is more important and what is less important. Your choices and decisions determine the entire structure and quality of your life. The only way you can get your life back into balance is by making different choices and different decisions.

The law of the excluded alternative says that doing one thing means *not* doing something else: every choice of a particular activity implies a rejection of all other choices and activities that you could do at the same time. Before you commit your time, you must think about what you will not be doing if you do something else.

The Power of Family Time

When you're with your family, be there 100 percent of the time. Leave things off. Resist the temptation to walk in the house at the end of the day and immediately turn on the television. As soon as the television goes on, all communication stops, and the entire focus of the family becomes the television screen. Don't let this happen to you and your family.

When you're with your family, take the time to give them what they need for emotional nourishment and support. As I've said, men and women are different in many ways. At the end of the day, men need acknowledgment for their work, appreciation for their efforts, an opportunity to explain what they have done during the day, and time to decompress. Women need attention, respect, affection, and listening. They need to talk and feel that the most important person in their life is listening to them respectfully.

Children need unconditional positive regard—acceptance, respect, attention, and especially the time of their parents. How does a child spell the word *love*? T-I-M-E.

The law of time in achieving work-life balance says that what counts is the quality of time at work, and the quantity of time at home. At work, you work on high-value, high-priority tasks so that you get a lot done and you're on top of things. At home, it is quantity of time, long unbroken quantities when you sit, talk, walk, and just spend time with the members of your family.

They say we live life by the years, but we experience it in the moments. You can never determine the exact moment when you're going to experience something wonderful with a member of your family. You have to allow lots of time for these unbidden moments to occur. Organize your personal life so that you spend ample time with the most important people. Take at least one full day off each week, during which you do no work at all. You only spend time with the members of your family or the important person in your life.

If you're married, take one three-day weekend off every three months to go away and spend time with your spouse. Take one- or two-week vacations twice each year, during which you do no work at all. This will help you get back into balance faster than almost anything else you can do.

Get Plenty of Rest

To get your life back into balance, you need plenty of rest: at least seven to eight hours each night. When you get too little sleep, you build up a sleep deficit, which causes you to go through the day in a fog. Because you're not thoroughly rested, you find it difficult to concentrate on the high-value activities that account for your success. Instead, because you're a little bit tired, you work on easier, lower-priority tasks that contribute little to your career.

Merely going to bed one hour early each night—getting one to two extra hours of sleep each night—can transform your life completely, and put your entire life back into balance.

Exercise two to three hundred minutes per week, even if all you do is go for a thirty- or forty-minute walk every day. This will increase your energy, improve your fitness, calm your mind, enable you to sleep better, and help bring your life back into balance. Even better, go for a walk with your spouse, or with one of your children; then you'll get multiple benefits from the same activity.

When you get your life into balance, you will feel terrific about yourself. You will get much more done at work and at home, you'll experience greater joy and satisfaction, and you'll be more successful in every part of your life.

Sometimes people ask me the secret to living a balanced life. I ask them this: how often does a tightrope walker balance when he is on the wire? All the time. The same is true for you. You don't achieve balance quickly and easily; it's something that you have to work at every single day.

The good news is that whatever you do repeatedly eventually becomes a habit. You can develop the habit of living a happy, high-performance, well-balanced life by simply practicing these ideas over and over until they become a regular part of your life.

13

Full Transformation

We've come a long way in our journey of transformation. Maybe you started out as someone who was directionless, dissatisfied with your life, feeling like a victim, and prone to blaming everyone else for your difficulties.

The first thing you learned is that it's pointless, and simply incorrect, to feel like a victim, because with your own mind, you have access to the most powerful force in the universe. You also learned that the first step to mastering this immense power is simply to focus your attention on what you want instead of what you don't want. This alone puts you ahead of the vast majority of people.

The next thing you learned was to motivate yourself toward peak performance through such powerful tools as optimism and exploring the boundless possibilities that are open to you. What if, for example, you could make ten times as much money as you're now making? Because of the power of the mind, simply focusing on this idea—even if you don't believe it at first—can start to bring it to reality.

Success has a great deal to do with self-motivation, but it's not enough. As we've seen, humans are social beings, and you will only achieve the goals you set for yourself by learning how to work with others and getting what you want from them—by helping them get what they want.

We also saw the importance of goal setting, which may be the single most important factor in bringing focus to your life. Setting goals, writing them down, and listing ways of accomplishing them is central to success. We also explored the most efficient way to move toward these goals—through optimal time management.

Then you learned the principles of wealth creation. Although it's important to do work that you love, your ultimate goal is full financial independence, so that you have plenty of money coming in whether you're working or not.

Of course, there are many paths to wealth creation, but statistically, the biggest one is through entrepreneurship—starting your own business. For the most part, the richest people in the world attained their wealth through starting their own businesses, and providing a product or service that was either unique or far superior to all the others. We've gone through some of the basic principles of entrepreneurship.

Next, we examined the fact that problems are a core part of life. No matter how healthy, wealthy, and successful you are, you will still face problems on a regular basis. Therefore, for a fully developed life, you need to understand how to face and solve problems.

Finally, we saw that the true goal of life is happiness, and for nearly all of us, happiness has to do with our relations with others. We saw how to simplify your life so that you have the time and energy for what really counts—which is almost always the people closest to you.

If you read, digest, and apply these principles, you can move from a life that may not be satisfying to one that is rich in all of the most important things. You can transform yourself from an ordinary bird into a splendid phoenix.

Let me conclude by repeating that we are living at the best time in human history. There are more opportunities and possibilities for you to live longer and better than ever existed before for any people on this earth. Your job is to take full advantage of this golden age of mankind to become everything that you are capable of becoming, to enjoy all the things that you ever dreamed of, and to live a long, happy life. I hope you do. Good luck.

CPSIA information can be obtained
at www.ICGtesting.com
Printed in the USA
JSHW052109080921
18546JS00003B/3